BELLA GEORGE

Madeira Hiking Guide 2024

*Explore Paradise on Foot, Your Madeira Hiking
Adventure Begins with Routes & Breathtaking Vistas*

First edition

This book was professionally typeset on Reedsy.
Find out more at reedsy.com

Contents

I

Introduction to Madeira Hiking

1

Welcome to Madeira: Unveiling the Island's Hiking Paradise

Madeira, a captivating Portuguese island nestled in the Atlantic Ocean, beckons you with a tapestry of dramatic coastlines that plunge into turquoise waters, verdant forests teeming with life, and majestic mountains that pierce the clouds. This volcanic gem, often dubbed the "Pearl of the Atlantic," is a haven for outdoor enthusiasts, particularly hikers who crave breathtaking vistas, diverse trails, and a chance to truly commune with nature.

This guidebook serves as your key to unlocking the magic of Madeira's hiking paradise. Whether you're a seasoned adventurer who has conquered peaks around the world or a curious first-timer eager to explore the wonders of the natural world, within these pages you'll discover something to ignite your wanderlust.

A Landscape Unlike Any Other: Delve into the island's unique geography, shaped by fiery volcanic eruptions millennia ago and sculpted by time into a wonderland of dramatic cliffs, hidden coves, and lush valleys. Explore the wonders of the Laurissilva forest, a UNESCO World Heritage Site teeming with ancient flora, some dating back to the Tertiary period. Witness a profusion of endemic species, like the vibrantly colored Madeira orchid or the rare Madeira laurel, that thrive in the island's unique microclimates.

A Paradise for All Levels: Unearth a network of trails catering to every skill level. From gentle levada walks, perfect for families with young children or those seeking a leisurely stroll amidst breathtaking scenery, to challenging mountain ascents that reward experienced hikers with panoramic vistas that stretch to the horizon, Madeira has something for everyone. Imagine strolling leisurely along a levada, an ingenious water irrigation system that winds its way through the island, enveloped by the emerald embrace of the Laurissilva forest and serenaded by the gentle murmur of cascading waterfalls. Or, for the more adventurous, picture yourself conquering Pico Ruivo, the highest peak on the island, and feeling the exhilaration of standing on top of the world, with breathtaking views of the entire island laid out before you.

Levada Wonderland: Immerse yourself in Madeira's unique levada system, a network of irrigation channels that snake their way for over 2,500 kilometers through the island's landscapes. These historic pathways, some dating back centuries, offer enchanting walks amidst lush vegetation and cascading waterfalls. Imagine traversing these gentle pathways, sunlight dappling through the leaves of towering eucalyptus trees, the refreshing scent of the forest filling your senses, and the sound of rushing water providing a natural soundtrack to your exploration. The levadas are more than just irrigation channels; they are the very lifeblood of Madeira, and a hike along their paths allows you to step back in time and appreciate the ingenuity of the islanders who built this remarkable network.

4

Beyond the Trails: Discover Madeira's rich cultural heritage, vibrant local cuisine, and charming villages. Learn about the island's fascinating history, dating back to the early explorers who first stumbled upon this volcanic paradise. Immerse yourself in the warm hospitality of the Madeiran people, known for their friendly smiles and welcoming spirit. Savor the flavors of the local cuisine, a delicious fusion of Portuguese and Mediterranean influences, featuring fresh seafood, exotic fruits, and the island's own volcanic wine, all enjoyed against the backdrop of stunning scenery. Explore the island's charming villages, where colorful houses adorned with flower-filled balconies line cobbled streets, and time seems to slow down, allowing you to truly appreciate the simple pleasures of life.

As you embark on your hiking adventure, this guidebook will be your trusted companion. We'll equip you with the essential knowledge and practical tips to ensure a safe, enjoyable, and unforgettable experience. Let us be your compass as you navigate Madeira's captivating landscapes, discover hidden treasures, and create memories that will last a lifetime.

1.1 Madeira's Unique Landscape and Hiking Culture: A Match Made in Paradise

Madeira's dramatic landscapes and rich hiking culture are intricately intertwined, offering a unique experience for outdoor enthusiasts. Here's a deeper dive into what makes this island a hiker's paradise:

A Volcanic Tapestry:

- **Volcanic Origins:** Millions of years of volcanic eruptions sculpted Madeira's diverse topography. Jagged peaks pierce the clouds, while lush valleys cradle charming villages. This volcanic legacy creates a stunning backdrop for your hikes.

- **Laurissilva Forest:** A UNESCO World Heritage Site, this ancient laurel forest is a relic from the Tertiary period. Imagine hiking amongst towering trees draped with emerald moss, a testament to the island's unique microclimates.
- **Levada Network:** A marvel of human ingenuity, this network of irrigation channels winds its way through the island, creating a unique hiking experience. Explore levadas lined with vibrant flowers and discover hidden waterfalls cascading down moss-covered rocks.

A Culture Steeped in Hiking:

- **Levadas: More Than Just Irrigation:** The levadas are deeply ingrained in Madeiran culture. Hiking these paths allows you to connect with the island's history and appreciate the resourcefulness of the islanders who built them.
- **Walking as a Way of Life:** Walking is a cherished activity in Madeira. From families enjoying leisurely strolls to locals commuting on foot, the island fosters a culture that embraces exploration on foot.
- **Veredas: Off-the-Beaten-Path Adventures:** Venture beyond the levadas and discover veredas, traditional hiking trails that lead you deeper into the island's wilderness. These paths offer a chance to experience the raw beauty of Madeira and encounter hidden gems.

Benefits of Hiking in Madeira:

- **Diverse Trails for All Levels:** Whether you're a seasoned hiker or a curious beginner, Madeira offers trails catering to all skill levels. Gentle levada walks are perfect for families, while challenging mountain ascents reward experienced hikers with breathtaking panoramas.

- **Year-Round Hiking:** Madeira's mild climate allows for year-round hiking. Escape the winter chill in Europe and enjoy pleasant temperatures perfect for outdoor adventures.
- **Unveiling Hidden Gems:** Hiking lets you discover Madeira beyond the tourist hotspots. Explore secluded coves, encounter cascading waterfalls, and stumble upon charming villages untouched by time.

Embrace the Spirit of Exploration:

As you embark on your hiking adventure in Madeira, remember, it's not just about reaching the destination. It's about savoring the journey, immersing yourself in the island's unique landscape, and connecting with the rich culture of hiking that thrives here. Let the vibrant flora, the refreshing scent of the Laurissilva forest, and the gentle murmur of water on the levadas guide your way. Madeira awaits with an unforgettable hiking experience!

1.2 Benefits of Hiking in Madeira: From Physical Activity to Cultural Immersion

Lace up your hiking boots and prepare to be invigorated by the multitude of benefits that Madeira's hiking trails offer. Here's why a hiking adventure in this volcanic paradise is more than just a walk in the park:

Physical and Mental Well-being:

- **Boost Your Fitness:** Hiking in Madeira's diverse terrain, from gentle inclines to challenging climbs, provides a fantastic cardiovascular workout. Immerse yourself in nature's gym and strengthen your body while enjoying breathtaking scenery.
- **Stress Relief and Mindfulness:** Escape the hustle and bustle of daily life and find serenity amidst the island's tranquil landscapes. The rhythmic sound of your steps on the trail, the fresh mountain air, and the captivating scenery all contribute to a sense of peace and well-being.
- **Increased Energy Levels:** Immersing yourself in nature is a proven way to boost energy levels. Sunshine exposure, fresh air, and physical activity all combine to leave you feeling revitalized and ready to explore more.

A Gateway to Cultural Immersion:

- **Connecting with History:** As you traverse the levadas, imagine the islanders who meticulously carved these channels centuries ago. Hike along veredas, traditional footpaths, and feel a connection to the island's historical walking culture.
- **Appreciating Local Craftsmanship:** Encounter "brancas," traditional stone houses, nestled amongst the hills, testaments to the island's unique architecture. Discover "bordados," intricate Madeira embroidery, a cherished local craft, and appreciate the island's artistic heritage.
- **Savoring Local Flavors:** After your hike, indulge in a delicious meal at a "tasquinha" (local tavern). Savor fresh seafood dishes, sample the island's volcanic wine, and experience the warmth of Madeiran hospitality.

A Deeper Connection with Nature:

- **A Paradise for Nature Lovers:** Madeira boasts a remarkable biodiversity. Encounter an array of endemic flora, like the vibrant Madeira orchid, and witness the unique fauna, including the trocaz pigeon, a bird found only in the Laurissilva forest.
- **Unveiling Hidden Treasures:** Hike beyond popular tourist destinations and discover secluded coves, cascading waterfalls, and hidden pockets of natural beauty. Embrace the feeling of discovery and appreciate the island's untouched landscapes.
- **Sustainable Exploration:** Hiking allows you to explore Madeira with minimal environmental impact. Leave no trace behind, respect the delicate ecosystems, and contribute to preserving this natural paradise for future generations.

Tailoring Your Experience:

The beauty of hiking in Madeira lies in its versatility. Whether you seek a challenging physical adventure or a relaxing stroll amidst breathtaking scenery, there's a trail waiting to be explored. Embrace the diverse benefits that Madeira's hikes offer and create a truly enriching experience that goes far beyond conquering a path.

1.3 Who Should Use This Guide: Matching Your Skills to the Perfect Trail

Madeira's hiking trails offer something for everyone, from families with young children to seasoned adventurers. This guide is designed to be your companion, regardless of your experience level. Here's how to find the perfect trail to match your skills and interests:

Hitting the Trails for the First Time?

- **Welcome, Beginner Hikers!** If you're new to hiking or have limited experience, Madeira offers a plethora of gentle levada walks perfect for you. These mostly flat paths with well-maintained surfaces are ideal for families with young children, stroller users, or those seeking a leisurely stroll.
- **Our Recommendations:** Look for trails marked as "fácil" (easy) in this guide. These routes are typically shorter in distance with minimal elevation gain, allowing you to enjoy the scenery at a relaxed pace. Some great options include:
- **Levada das 25 Fontes:** An enchanting walk through Laurissilva forest with multiple waterfalls.
- **Balcões Viewpoint:** A short hike with breathtaking panoramic views of the Ribeira Brava Valley.

Calling All Adventure Enthusiasts!

- **Are You an Intermediate Hiker?** If you have some hiking experience and are looking for a moderate challenge, Madeira has you covered. Trails with moderate inclines and varied terrain will provide a good workout while offering stunning vistas.

- **Get Your Heart Pumping:** Look for trails marked as "moderado" (moderate) in this guide. These routes offer a bit more distance and elevation gain, making for a more adventurous experience. Some exciting options include:
- **Caldeirão Verde**: Hike through the heart of the Laurissilva forest, a UNESCO World Heritage Site.
- **Queimadas Forest:** Explore a network of levadas amidst vineyards and traditional villages.

Conquer the Peaks: Seasoned Hikers Welcome!

- **Ready for a Challenge?** For experienced hikers seeking a strenuous adventure, Madeira boasts mountain ascents with breathtaking rewards. These trails require a good level of fitness, proper gear, and a sense of adventure.
- **Challenge Yourself:** Look for trails marked as "difícil" (difficult) in this guide. These routes involve significant elevation gain, steep inclines, and potentially technical terrain. Be sure to plan accordingly and prioritize safety. Some challenging options include:
- **Pico do Arieiro:** Ascend Madeira's third-highest peak and witness panoramic island views.
- **PR 9 Levada da Serra do Faial:** A challenging hike with sections that require scrambling and offer stunning landscapes.

Beyond Skill Level: Considering Your Interests

In addition to skill level, consider your interests when choosing a trail. This guide highlights specific trails known for:

- **Waterfalls:** Hunt for cascading waterfalls along routes like Levada do Caniçal.

- **Panoramic Views:** Ascend Pico Ruivo for unparalleled vistas or explore shorter options with viewpoints like Balcões.
- **Local Villages:** Integrate hikes with visits to charming villages like those found near Queimadas Forest.
- **Family-Friendly Adventures:** Prioritize gentle levada walks with manageable inclines and even terrain, like Levada das 25 Fontes.

Remember: Safety is paramount. Always choose a trail that matches your skill level and physical condition. Be sure to research specific routes before you embark, check weather conditions, and let someone know your planned itinerary.

   With this guide and a little planning, you're sure to find the perfect trail to match your skills and ignite your passion for hiking in Madeira!

2

Planning Your Madeira Hiking Adventure

Madeira, the "Pearl of the Atlantic," is a volcanic island paradise waiting to be explored by foot. With its dramatic coastlines, lush forests, and soaring peaks, Madeira offers a diverse range of hikes for all levels of experience. This chapter will guide you through everything you need to plan your unforgettable Madeira hiking adventure.

Step 1: Choosing Your Hike

Madeira boasts an extensive network of levadas (ancient irrigation channels) that have been transformed into scenic walking paths. Here's how to find the perfect hike:

- **Skill Level:** Consider your fitness level and hiking experience. Madeira offers hikes ranging from gentle strolls along levadas to challenging ascents to mountain peaks.
- **Duration:** Decide how much time you want to spend hiking. Hikes range from short loops to multi-day treks.
- **Location:** Madeira is divided into south and north regions. The south is generally drier and sunnier, while the north is lusher and wetter. Choose a location that suits your

preferences and itinerary.

- **Interests:** Do you crave panoramic views? Seek out levada walks along mountain ridges. Are you a waterfall enthusiast? Look for hikes that lead to cascading beauties.

Step 2: Researching Your Hike

Once you've chosen a hike, delve deeper into the specifics:

- **Difficulty Rating:** Most trails have a signage system indicating difficulty. Familiarize yourself with the rating system and choose accordingly.
- **Trail Descriptions:** Utilize online resources like https://visitmadeira.com/en/what-to-do/nature-seekers/activities/hiking/ or guidebooks to find detailed descriptions, elevation profiles, and estimated walking times.
- **Permits and Fees:** A few trails, particularly those in natural reserves, may require permits or entrance fees. Check local tourist information centers for details.

Step 3: Gearing Up

- **Footwear:** Sturdy hiking boots with good ankle support are essential for uneven terrain.
- **Clothing:** Dress in layers for changeable weather. Pack waterproof outerwear, a hat, and sunscreen.
- **Essentials:** Don't forget a backpack, refillable water bottle, snacks, first-aid kit, and a map or GPS device. Download offline maps in case of limited phone reception.

Step 4: Booking Accommodation and Transportation

- **Accommodation:** Madeira offers a variety of accommodation options, from hotels in Funchal (the capital) to rural guesthouses nestled amidst the mountains. Consider your desired location and proximity to your chosen hikes.
- **Transportation:** Public buses connect most towns and villages. Renting a car offers flexibility, especially if you plan to explore a variety of trails across the island.

Step 5: Additional Tips

- **Weather:** Madeira's weather can be unpredictable. Check forecasts before your hike and be prepared for sudden changes.
- **Respect the Environment:** Stick to designated trails, avoid littering, and be mindful of local flora and fauna.
- **Embrace the Culture:** Sample Madeiran cuisine after your hike. Enjoy a refreshing drink at a local café and soak in the island's charm.

By following these steps and keeping these tips in mind, you can ensure a safe, enjoyable, and unforgettable hiking adventure in Madeira.

Bonus: Consider hiring a local guide, especially for challenging hikes or if you'd like to learn more about the island's natural history and culture.

2.1 Deciding When to Hike: Madeira's Seasonal Variations and Ideal Hiking Months

Madeira's nickname, the "Pearl of the Atlantic," applies to its hiking trails as much as anything else. While you can lace up your boots year-round, the island's distinct seasons offer different advantages to hikers seeking the perfect experience.

- **Spring (April-May):** Spring paints Madeira in vibrant hues. Wildflowers burst into bloom, transforming trails into colorful corridors. Pleasant temperatures with warm days and cool nights make hiking comfortable for extended periods. Spring also falls under the shoulder season, meaning you'll encounter fewer crowds compared to the peak summer months. This sweet spot between pleasant weather and manageable crowds makes spring a favorite time for many hikers.
- **Summer (June-August):** Summer in Madeira bathes the island in sunshine, making it ideal for hikers who love warm weather and clear skies. If you enjoy soaking up the sun while conquering trails, summer offers the most daylight hours for your adventures. However, the afternoon heat can be intense, so be sure to start your hikes early and pack plenty of water. Crowds tend to swell during peak summer months, so be prepared for company on popular trails.
- **Autumn (September-October):** As summer wanes, autumn offers another shoulder season with comfortable temperatures. The initial flush of summer crowds has thinned, making trails feel less crowded. While the chance of rain increases slightly compared to spring, Madeira generally enjoys drier weather than winter. Lush green landscapes

transition into fiery hues, creating a visually stunning backdrop for your hikes.

- **Winter (November-March):** Madeira boasts the mildest winter in Europe. Rain is more frequent during these months, and there's a possibility of snow at higher elevations. While hiking is still possible throughout winter, some trails may be slippery or closed due to weather conditions. However, winter offers a unique advantage for waterfall enthusiasts – the increased rainfall translates to cascading waterfalls at their most powerful. Just be sure to pack proper footwear and clothing with good waterproofing for winter hikes.

In a nutshell:

- **Shoulder Seasons (Spring & Autumn):** Ideal for pleasant weather and fewer crowds.
- **Summer:** Perfect for sunshine and warmth, but be prepared for hot afternoons and potentially larger crowds.
- **Winter:** Offers the chance to witness waterfalls at their fullest, but be aware of increased rain and potential trail closures.

No matter the season: Madeira's weather can be unpredictable. Always check the forecast before your hike and pack accordingly to ensure a safe and enjoyable experience.

2.2 Choosing Your Accommodation: Hiking-Friendly Locations and Amenities

After picking the perfect hike, finding the right place to stay is key to a successful Madeira hiking adventure. Here's how to choose accommodation that complements your hiking ambitions:

Location, Location, Location!

- **Centralized Hub:** Funchal, Madeira's capital, offers a wide range of hotels and hostels. It's a great base if you plan to explore various trails across the island and rely on public transportation. However, be prepared for commutes to trailheads.
- **Hiking Hotspot Villages:** Consider staying in villages nestled amidst the mountains, like Santana or Porto Moniz. These locations put you right on the doorstep of many popular hikes, eliminating the need for long commutes. Explore the charming town of Santana known for its traditional thatched-roof houses after a day conquering levada walks. Immerse yourself in the natural beauty of Porto Moniz, a village famed for its volcanic black sand beach, after tackling the challenging hike to Pico Ruivo, the highest peak on Madeira.
- **Rural Charm:** Opt for a traditional "quinta" (farmhouse) or guesthouse in rural areas. These accommodations often boast breathtaking mountain views and a tranquil atmosphere, perfect for unwinding after a day on the trails. Imagine soaking in the sunset over the valley from your balcony after a refreshing dip in the quinta's natural pool.

Amenities for Hikers

- **Drying Facilities:** Look for accommodation with drying racks or laundry services, especially if you plan on multi-day hikes or anticipate encountering wet weather. Having damp boots and clothes can put a damper on your post-hike relaxation.
- **Secure Gear Storage:** Having a secure place to store your hiking boots, backpack, and other gear is essential. Inquire about lockers or designated storage areas, especially if your chosen accommodation doesn't have individual rooms that can lock.
- **Packed Lunches:** Some hotels and guesthouses offer packed lunch options, ideal for fueling your hikes without the need for early morning grocery runs. This allows you to grab a delicious and convenient meal to take with you on the trails, maximizing your time to explore.

Bonus Considerations

- **Relaxation Options:** After a long day on the trails, having access to a spa, swimming pool, or hot tub can be a welcome luxury. Consider these amenities when choosing your accommodation. Imagine soothing your tired muscles in a hot tub overlooking the mountains after conquering a challenging levada walk.
- **Local Recommendations:** Friendly guesthouse owners or hotel staff can be a wealth of knowledge when it comes to hidden hiking gems or lesser-known trails. Don't hesitate to ask for recommendations! Local insights can lead you to discover off-the-beaten-path adventures you might have

otherwise missed.

By considering these factors, you can find accommodation that perfectly complements your hiking itinerary and sets the stage for a comfortable and fulfilling Madeira hiking experience. Imagine waking up to fresh mountain air, enjoying a delicious breakfast fueled by local ingredients, and then venturing out to explore the island's diverse trails, knowing you have a cozy and welcoming place to return to at the end of the day.

2.3 Essential Gear and Packing List: Preparing for Comfort and Safety on the Trails

Conquering Madeira's trails is an exhilarating experience, but proper preparation is key to ensuring both comfort and safety. Here's a comprehensive list of essential gear to pack for your hiking adventures:

Footwear:

- **Hiking Boots:** Sturdy, waterproof hiking boots with good ankle support are paramount. Uneven terrain and potential for wet or muddy conditions necessitate proper footwear.

Clothing:

- **Base Layer:** Opt for a moisture-wicking base layer to keep you comfortable during exertion.
- **Hiking Pants:** Choose quick-drying, breathable hiking pants that allow for freedom of movement.
- **Insulating Layer:** Pack a fleece or light jacket for cooler temperatures or unexpected weather changes.

- **Rain Jacket:** A waterproof and windproof rain jacket is crucial for unpredictable island weather.
- **Hat:** A wide-brimmed hat protects you from the sun and helps regulate body temperature.
- **Sun Protection:** Pack sunscreen with a high SPF rating to shield your skin from the sun's rays.

Hydration and Nutrition:

- **Backpack:** Choose a comfortable backpack with sufficient capacity to carry all your essentials for the day. Consider features like adjustable straps and good ventilation.
- **Water Bottle:** Bring a refillable water bottle of at least 1 liter to stay hydrated throughout your hike. Opt for an insulated bottle if hiking during hot weather.
- **Snacks:** Pack high-energy snacks like nuts, granola bars, or dried fruit to keep you fueled on the trails.

Navigation and Safety:

- **Map and Compass (or GPS Device):** Even with marked trails, having a map and compass (or a downloaded offline GPS app) can be a lifesaver if you get lost. Familiarize yourself with using these tools before your hike.
- **First-Aid Kit:** Pack a basic first-aid kit containing essential supplies like bandages, antiseptic wipes, pain relievers, and any personal medications you might need.
- **Headlamp or Torch:** A headlamp or torch is essential, especially if you plan on exploring tunnels along levada walks or anticipate finishing your hike after dark.
- **Whistle:** A whistle can be a valuable tool to attract attention

in case of an emergency.

Additional Considerations:

- **Sunglasses:** Protect your eyes from the sun's glare with a good pair of sunglasses.
- **Cash:** Carrying some cash can be helpful for buying snacks or drinks at local cafes you might encounter along the trails.
- **Camera:** Capture the beauty of Madeira's landscapes with a camera. A waterproof case is recommended in case of rain.
- **Hiking Poles (Optional):** Hiking poles can offer additional support and stability, especially on challenging terrain or steep climbs.

Packing Tips:

- Layer your clothing so you can adjust to changing weather conditions.
- Pack a lightweight rain cover for your backpack to protect your gear from sudden showers.
- Wear comfortable shoes for the journey to and from the trailhead.
- Don't forget important documents like your passport and travel insurance information.

By packing this essential gear and following these tips, you'll be well-equipped to tackle Madeira's trails with confidence and comfort, allowing you to focus on enjoying the breathtaking scenery and the thrill of the hike. Remember, a little planning goes a long way in ensuring a safe and unforgettable Madeira hiking adventure.

2.4 Understanding Trail Difficulty Levels and Grading Systems in Madeira

Madeira caters to hikers of all abilities, with trails ranging from gentle strolls along levadas to challenging ascents up mountain peaks. The key to choosing the perfect hike is understanding Madeira's trail difficulty grading system. Here's what you need to know:

The PR Marking System

Madeira's trails are categorized using the **PR (Portuguese Caminho Real - Royal Way)** markings system. These markings are typically yellow and red stripes painted on rocks or posts along the trail. The difficulty level is indicated by a number and color combination:

- **0 - PR (sarı)** (Yellow): **Easy** - Suitable for all ages and fitness levels. Mostly flat or gentle slopes. These are excellent choices for families with young children or those seeking a leisurely stroll through scenic landscapes.
- **1 - PR (verde)** (Green): **Moderate** - May involve some steeper sections and uneven terrain. Requires a moderate level of fitness. These are good options for those who are comfortable with some inclines and are in reasonable physical condition.
- **2 - PR (azul)** (Blue): **Challenging** - Demanding hikes with steeper climbs, uneven surfaces, and potentially exposed sections. Good fitness and surefootedness required. These trails are best suited for experienced hikers who are comfortable with navigating challenging terrain.
- **3 - PR (vermelho)** (Red): **Very Challenging** - Strenuous hikes with significant elevation gain, rough terrain, and

potential for long distances. Requires excellent fitness and experience. Only attempt these trails if you are a very fit and experienced hiker who is comfortable with technical terrain.

Beyond the PR System

While the PR system provides a general guideline, it's important to consider additional factors before choosing a hike:

- **Total Distance:** Even a relatively easy (yellow) trail can be tiring if it covers a long distance. Be sure to consider the total length of the hike in addition to the difficulty rating.
- **Elevation Gain:** Significant elevation gain can make a hike more challenging, even on well-maintained trails. Be mindful of the elevation profile when choosing a hike.
- **Technical Terrain:** Some trails may involve sections with loose rocks, scrambles, or narrow passages. These elements can increase the difficulty of a hike, even if the overall elevation gain is low.

Finding Detailed Trail Information

Always consult detailed trail descriptions before embarking on your hike. Here are some valuable resources:

- The official Madeira tourism website provides descriptions and difficulty ratings for many popular trails.
- https://numi.world/a-hikers-guide-to-hiking-madeira/) – A website by a hiker offering detailed trail information and reviews.
- **Trail Apps:** Several apps, such as Wikiloc or AllTrails, offer user-generated trail information and reviews, including

difficulty ratings.

By familiarizing yourself with the PR system, considering additional factors, and consulting detailed trail information, you can choose hikes in Madeira that are a perfect match for your fitness level and experience, ensuring a safe and enjoyable adventure.

3

Essential Information for Hikers in Madeira

Having planned your trip, chosen your hike, and packed your gear, here's some vital information to ensure a safe and enjoyable hiking experience in Madeira:

Trail Etiquette and Safety

- **Respect the Island:** Stay on designated trails to avoid damaging the island's delicate ecosystems and wildlife. Pack out all your trash and leave no trace behind. Madeira's natural beauty is a treasure, treat it with care so future hikers can enjoy it as well.

- **Trail Courtesy:** Hikers going downhill typically have the right of way. Step aside to allow them to pass safely, especially on narrow sections of the trail. Common courtesy goes a long way in creating a pleasant experience for everyone sharing the trails.

- **Watch Your Step:** Be mindful of loose rocks, especially on steeper inclines. Dislodging rocks can be dangerous for hikers below. Trekking poles can also provide additional stability and help you navigate uneven terrain.

- **Tunnel Awareness:** Some levada walks involve tunnels. Use a headlamp or torch and watch out for uneven surfaces or potential water on the floor. These tunnels can be exciting adventures, but proper lighting is essential to ensure safe passage.
- **Be Weather Wise:** Madeira's weather can change rapidly. Check the forecast before your hike and be prepared for sudden downpours or strong winds. Don't attempt hikes exceeding your ability in poor weather. Madeira's unique location can result in unpredictable conditions, so dressing in layers and being prepared for anything is crucial.
- **Share Your Plans:** Inform your accommodation or a friend about your hiking itinerary, especially if venturing on re-mote trails. This can provide peace of mind and allow for assistance if needed.

Helpful Resources and Apps

- **Madeira Tourism Website:** https://visitmadeira.com/en/ - Find official information on trails, maps, weather, and safety recommendations. This website is a comprehensive resource for all things hiking in Madeira.
- **Emergency Help:** Dial 112 for assistance in case of an emergency. Knowing the emergency number is essential for any outdoor activity.
- **Offline Maps:** Download offline maps and trail information for your chosen hikes in case of limited mobile reception on the trails. Consider apps like Maps.me or Google Maps. Having offline resources ensures you can stay on track even if you lose cell service.

- **Hiking Apps:** Utilize apps like Wikiloc or AllTrails for user-generated trail information, reviews, and GPS navigation features. These apps can provide valuable insights from other hikers and help you navigate the trails with confidence.

Additional Tips

- **Learn a Few Phrases:** A few basic Portuguese phrases like "Obrigada" (thank you) or "Bom dia" (good morning) can be appreciated by locals you meet on the trails. It's a gesture of respect for the local culture and can enhance your interactions with Madeiran people.
- **Embrace the Culture:** Sample Madeiran cuisine after your hike. Enjoy a refreshing drink at a local café and soak in the island's charm. You might discover hidden culinary gems or local traditions. Madeira has a rich cultural heritage, and exploring the local food and customs can add another dimension to your hiking adventure.
- **Support Local Businesses:** Consider purchasing locally-made souvenirs or enjoying meals at family-run restaurants in the villages you explore. This supports the local economy and adds an authentic touch to your trip. Your tourist dollars can help sustain the communities that preserve Madeira's unique character.

With this essential information, you're well on your way to an unforgettable hiking adventure in Madeira. Happy hiking! May your trails be scenic, your legs be strong, and your memories be everlasting!

3.1 Levadas: The Heart of Madeira's Hiking Network - History, Types, and Etiquette

Levadas are the beating heart of Madeira's hiking trails. These unique irrigation channels, winding their way through lush valleys and dramatic mountainsides, offer a captivating way to explore the island's stunning scenery. This section delves into the history, types, and proper etiquette for enjoying these remarkable pathways.

A Legacy of Resourcefulness:

- **Born from Necessity:** Madeira's volcanic origin resulted in a naturally uneven distribution of water. The island's south is drier, while the north receives more rainfall. Centuries ago, resourceful Madeirans constructed levadas to channel water from the rainy north to the fertile south, nurturing agricultural endeavors. These ingenious channels have become an integral part of the island's cultural heritage and continue to play a vital role in irrigation today. Imagine the backbreaking labor involved in carving these channels by hand through volcanic rock, a testament to the determination and ingenuity of the Madeiran people.

A Variety of Levadas:

- **Main Levadas (Levadas Mães):** These larger channels, typically constructed in the 15th and 16th centuries, are the backbone of the irrigation system. They often flow through tunnels carved by hand, showcasing the impressive engineering feats of the past. While some main levadas are not suitable for walking due to their size and water flow, they

29

form the foundation of the network of hiking trails. Imagine walking alongside a levada mãe, the sound of rushing water a constant companion, and catching glimpses of the original hand-hewn carvings in the tunnel walls, offering a window into Madeira's rich history.

· **Veredas:** These are smaller levada branches that divert water from the main channels to agricultural terraces. Veredas are often narrower and steeper than main levadas, offering a more adventurous hiking experience. They may also wind through more secluded areas, providing a chance to truly immerse yourself in the island's verdant landscapes.

· **Balaúço Levadas:** These unique levadas feature sections built on stilts, allowing the water to navigate steep cliffs and ravines. Walking along a levada balanceiro can be an exhilarating experience, offering breathtaking views and a true sense of adventure. Imagine the feeling of walking on a narrow channel suspended above a lush valley, the cool mist rising from the levada below, and the panoramic vistas unfolding before you – an unforgettable experience that combines nature's beauty with human ingenuity.

Hiking Etiquette on Levadas:

· **Respect the Flow:** Be mindful of the levada's primary function – irrigation. Avoid blocking the water flow or contaminating it with litter or waste. The levadas are a vital resource for the island's agriculture, so treat them with respect.

· **Single File on Narrow Stretches:** When navigating narrow sections, step aside to allow hikers coming from the opposite direction to pass safely. Single file walking ensures a smooth flow of traffic on the trails, especially considering the levadas can vary in width, and some sections may only accommodate one person at a time.

- **Leash Your Dog:** If hiking with a dog, keep it leashed and under control to avoid disturbing other hikers or wildlife. The levadas are home to a variety of birdlife and other creatures, and keeping your dog leashed helps protect the ecosystem and ensures a safe and enjoyable experience for everyone.

- **Enjoy the Silence:** The levadas offer a tranquil escape into nature. Avoid loud noises and be mindful of other hikers seeking a peaceful experience. The sound of rushing water and the calls of birds create a natural symphony on the levada walks. Respect the tranquility of the environment and listen to the music of Madeira.

By understanding the history and types of levadas, and following proper etiquette, you can ensure a respectful and enjoyable hiking experience while appreciating these remarkable feats of engineering and cultural heritage. The levadas await you, ready to unveil the hidden beauty of Madeira, steeped in history, surrounded by nature, and offering a unique glimpse into the soul of the island.

3.2 Permits and Regulations: Responsible Hiking Practices and Access Requirements

Madeira's stunning landscapes are a hiker's paradise, but with great trails come a few responsibilities. This section explores the island's permit and regulation system, ensuring you explore responsibly and ethically.

Hiking with Awareness:

- **Leave No Trace:** As mentioned earlier, adhering to the principles of Leave No Trace is paramount. Pack out all your trash and avoid disturbing the natural environment. Madeira's beauty thrives on responsible tourism, so minimize your impact and leave the trails as pristine as you found them.
- **Respect Wildlife:** Madeira boasts a unique ecosystem with various bird species, butterflies, and other creatures. Maintain a safe distance from wildlife and avoid disrupting their habitats. Hikers who appreciate and respect the wildlife will be rewarded with potential sightings of these fascinating creatures in their natural environment.
- **Fire Safety:** Madeira's summers can be dry, so be extremely cautious with fire. Never leave campfires unattended and extinguish them properly before leaving the area. A single spark can have devastating consequences, so prioritize fire safety to protect the island's natural treasures.

Permits and Restricted Areas:

- **Generally Permit-Free:** The majority of Madeira's levada walks and hiking trails are free to access and don't require permits. However, a few exceptions exist.

- **Natural Reserves:** Some designated natural reserves may have specific regulations or require permits for entry. Always check with local tourist information centers or park authorities before venturing into protected areas. These permits are often minimal fees that contribute to conservation efforts and responsible park management.
- **Restricted Areas:** Certain areas, like some mountain peaks or nesting grounds for endangered birds, may be restricted for safety or conservation purposes. Respect all posted signage and avoid entering restricted zones. Following designated trails and respecting restricted areas ensures your safety and the preservation of Madeira's delicate ecosystems.

Responsible Practices:

- **Parking Considerately:** Parking can be limited in some trailhead areas. Park only in designated spots and avoid blocking traffic or private driveways. Being a considerate parker helps maintain a smooth flow for everyone and avoids any inconvenience to local residents.
- **Public Toilets:** Public restrooms are not always readily available on hiking trails. Plan accordingly and utilize facilities when available to avoid leaving any waste behind in natural areas.
- **Support Local Businesses:** Opt for local restaurants and shops in the villages you explore. This injects tourism dollars directly into the local economy and supports the communities that maintain the hiking trails and preserve Madeira's unique character.

By following these regulations and adopting responsible prac-tices, you can become a steward of Madeira's natural beauty. Your mindful actions contribute to a sustainable future for the island's trails and ensure future generations can enjoy these remarkable landscapes. Happy hiking, and remember, tread lightly and leave Madeira a little wilder than you found it!

3.3 Transportation Options: Getting Around Madeira and Reaching Trailheads

Exploring Madeira's diverse landscapes often requires navigat-ing from your accommodation to various trailheads. Here's a breakdown of your transportation options for a seamless hiking adventure:

Rental Car:

- **Flexibility and Freedom:** Renting a car offers the most flexibility for exploring Madeira at your own pace. You can create a customized itinerary, reach remote trailheads, and stop at scenic viewpoints along the way.
- **Convenience:** Pick up your car upon arrival at Funchal Airport and enjoy the comfort of having your own trans-portation throughout your trip.
- **Challenges:** Be aware of potentially narrow and winding roads, especially in mountainous areas. Parking can also be limited at some trailheads. Research parking options in advance, especially for popular hikes.

Public Buses:

- **Budget-Friendly:** Public buses are a cost-effective way to get around Madeira, especially if you're traveling solo or on a tight budget. The network covers most major towns and villages.

- **Planning Required:** Bus schedules may not always align perfectly with your desired hiking times. Research timetables and potential wait times in advance to avoid delays.
- **Limited Reach:** Remote trailheads may not be accessible by public bus. In such cases, consider combining buses with taxis or exploring alternative hikes closer to bus routes.

Taxis:

- **Convenience and Comfort:** Taxis offer a comfortable and convenient option for reaching trailheads, especially if you don't want to deal with car rentals or limited bus schedules.
- **Cost Considerations:** Taxis can be more expensive than other options, especially for longer distances. Agree on the fare with the driver beforehand to avoid any surprises.
- **Availability:** Taxis may not always be readily available in remote areas. It's wise to book a taxi in advance, especially if you require transportation after your hike.

Organized Tours:

- **All-Inclusive Experience:** Some tour companies offer guided hiking tours that include transportation, picnics, and sometimes even entrance fees to natural reserves.
- **Stress-Free Exploration:** Guided tours take care of the logistics, allowing you to focus on enjoying the scenery and learning from experienced guides.
- **Limited Flexibility:** You'll be following the tour itinerary

and schedule, with less freedom to explore at your own pace.

Choosing the Right Option:

The best transportation option depends on your individual preferences, budget, and the specific hikes you plan to conquer.

- **For maximum flexibility and freedom, a rental car is ideal.**
- **Budget-minded hikers can explore the well-covered areas using public buses.**
- **Taxis offer a convenient option for reaching remote trailheads or for those who prefer not to drive.**
- **Consider guided tours if you prefer a stress-free experience with all logistics handled.**

No matter your chosen mode of transportation, remember to factor in travel time when planning your hiking itinerary. Allow ample time to reach the trailhead, accounting for potential delays or limited bus schedules. With a little planning and the right transportation option, you'll be on your way to exploring the wonders of Madeira's many trails.

3.4 Safety on the Trails: Emergency Numbers, Weather Considerations, and Sun Protection

Conquering Madeira's trails is an exhilarating experience, but safety should always be your top priority. Here are some crucial tips to ensure a safe and enjoyable adventure:

Emergency Numbers:

- **112:** This is the single European emergency number. Remember this number and dial it immediately in case of an accident or serious medical emergency.

Weather Awareness:

- **Check the Forecast:** Madeira's weather can change rapidly. Always consult the forecast before your hike and be prepared for sudden downpours, strong winds, or fog. Don't underestimate the power of these elements, and adjust your plans accordingly.
- **Dress in Layers:** Layering allows you to adapt to changing weather conditions. Pack a waterproof jacket, even if the forecast predicts sunshine. Mountain weather can be unpredictable, and being prepared for rain is essential.
- **Sturdy Footwear:** Wear sturdy hiking boots with good ankle support for uneven terrain and potential slippery conditions, especially after rain. Proper footwear is crucial to avoid slips, falls, and injuries.

Sun Protection:

- **Sunscreen:** Madeira's sunshine can be intense, especially at higher altitudes. Apply sunscreen with a high SPF rating (SPF 30 or higher) generously and reapply throughout the day, especially after sweating or swimming.
- **Sun Hat:** Protect your head and face from the sun's harmful rays with a wide-brimmed hat.
- **Sunglasses:** A good pair of sunglasses is essential to shield your eyes from the glare and protect them from UV rays.

Additional Safety Tips:

- **Inform Others:** Let your accommodation or a friend know your hiking itinerary, especially if venturing on remote trails. This allows them to raise the alarm if you don't return as expected.
- **Stay Hydrated:** Bring a sufficient amount of water and drink regularly throughout your hike, even if you don't feel thirsty. Dehydration can set in quickly, especially in warm weather.
- **Pack a Headlamp:** If your hike extends beyond daylight hours, or if you plan on exploring tunnels along levada walks, pack a headlamp to ensure proper visibility.
- **Be Aware of Surroundings:** Pay attention to your surroundings and watch out for loose rocks, uneven terrain, or potential hazards on the trail.
- **Know Your Limits:** Choose hikes that match your fitness level and experience. Don't attempt trails beyond your capabilities, especially in challenging weather conditions.

By following these safety precautions and adopting a responsible approach, you can minimize risks and ensure a worry-free hiking experience in Madeira. Remember, safety is paramount. Embrace the adventure, but prioritize your well-being, and don't hesitate to turn back if weather conditions worsen or the trail becomes too difficult. Madeira's trails await you, but they should be explored with a cautious and prepared mind. Happy hiking!

II

Exploring Madeira's Diverse Hiking Trails

4

West Madeira - Dramatic Coastlines and Lush Laurissilva Forests

West Madeira is a hiker's paradise, offering a diverse landscape of dramatic coastlines, soaring cliffs, and verdant forests. This region boasts some of the island's most stunning scenery, with trails catering to all experience levels. From gentle levada walks amidst the UNESCO-listed Laurissilva Forest to challenging ascents up mountain peaks, western Madeira promises an unforgettable hiking adventure.

Highlights of Western Madeira:

- **Seixal and Ribeira da Casas:** Explore the charming village of Seixal, known for its natural black sand beach and volcanic rock pools. Hike along the levadas that wind through the Ribeira da Casas valley, surrounded by lush Laurissilva Forest.
- **Paul da Serra Plateau:** Venture into the Paul da Serra plateau, a hiker's haven boasting breathtaking panoramic views. Explore levada walks amidst a blanket of *Juniperus* trees, endemic to Madeira.

- **Fanal Laurissilva Forest:** Immerse yourself in the UNESCO World Heritage Laurissilva Forest, a primeval ecosystem teeming with endemic flora. Hike along the Levada do Balcão trails, offering enchanting scenery and unique biodiversity.
- **Cabo Girão**: Europe's highest cliff viewpoint offers breathtaking panoramas of the Atlantic Ocean. Hike along the trails leading to the viewpoint and challenge yourself with the skywalk suspended over the cliff edge.

Planning Your West Madeira Hiking Adventure:

- **Accommodation:** Consider basing yourself in villages like Seixal, Porto Moniz, or Calheta, offering easy access to western Madeira's trails. Opt for a traditional "quinta" (farmhouse) for a unique Madeiran experience.
- **Transportation:** Renting a car provides the most flexibility for exploring western Madeira's diverse locations. Alternatively, public buses connect the main villages, but reaching some trailheads may require taxis or joining organized tours.
- **Weather:** Western Madeira experiences slightly more rainfall than the island's south. Check the forecast before your hike and be prepared for potential rain showers. Dress in layers and waterproof gear to adapt to changing weather conditions.

Essential Gear:

- **Hiking boots:** Sturdy footwear with good ankle support is crucial for the uneven terrain of western Madeira's trails.

- **Rain jacket:** A waterproof jacket is essential for sudden downpours, especially in higher altitude areas.
- **Sun protection:** Sunscreen, sunglasses, and a hat are vital for sunny days.
- **Water bottle:** Stay hydrated by bringing a refillable water bottle on your hikes.
- **Headlamp:** A headlamp is necessary if you plan on exploring tunnels along levada walks or anticipate finishing your hike after dark.

Sustainable Hiking Practices:

- **Respect the environment:** Stick to designated trails to avoid damaging the fragile ecosystem. Leave no trace and pack out all your trash.
- **Support local communities:** Dine at local restaurants and purchase souvenirs from local artisans in the villages you explore. This supports the communities that preserve Madeira's natural beauty.
- **Be mindful of wildlife:** Madeira boasts a variety of birdlife and other creatures. Maintain a safe distance from wildlife and avoid disrupting their habitats.

With its dramatic coastlines, verdant forests, and diverse hiking trails, western Madeira beckons outdoor enthusiasts from across the globe. By following these recommendations, you can plan an unforgettable and enriching hiking adventure in this remarkable corner of Madeira. So lace up your boots, grab your backpack, and get ready to explore the magic of western Madeira!

4.1 Levada das 25 Fontes: A Family-Friendly Walk Through Lush Vegetation

The Levada das 25 Fontes, also known as the 25 Fountains Levada, is a picturesque and relatively easy hike perfect for families with children. This enchanting route winds through Madeira's Laurissilva Forest, a UNESCO World Heritage Site, offering a delightful introduction to the island's natural beauty.

Enchanting Waterfalls and Lush Landscapes:

The Levada das 25 Fontes translates to "Levada of the 25 Fountains," and the name perfectly captures the hike's highlight. As you follow the levada, you'll encounter 25 small waterfalls cascading down moss-covered rocks, creating a magical scene. The constant sound of trickling water and the vibrant green foliage will immerse you in the tranquility of the Laurissilva Forest.

Suitable for All Ages:

The Levada das 25 Fontes is a relatively flat and well-maintained path, making it suitable for hikers of all ages and fitness levels. The gentle incline and wide paths allow families with young children or grandparents to comfortably enjoy the walk. Relaxing picnic spots along the way provide opportunities to rest, admire the scenery, and refuel with snacks.

Distance and Duration:

The Levada das 25 Fontes is a linear out-and-back trail, with a total distance of approximately 4.3 kilometers (2.7 miles). Depending on your pace and the number of breaks you take, completing the hike can take anywhere from 2 to 3 hours. The leisurely pace allows families to explore the surroundings, take photos, and truly appreciate the beauty of the levada.

Reaching the 25 Fontes Waterfall:

The official endpoint of the Levada das 25 Fontes is the waterfall itself. A short, steeper section leads you to a viewing platform offering breathtaking vistas of the cascading water surrounded by lush vegetation. While the main path is easily manageable, this final section requires a bit more care, especially for young children. Here, adult supervision is crucial to ensure everyone's safety.

Tips for a Family Hike:

- **Start Early:** Especially during peak season, starting your hike early allows you to avoid crowds and ensures a more peaceful experience.
- **Pack Essentials:** Bring plenty of water, snacks, sunscreen, hats, and comfortable shoes for the entire family.
- **Engage the Children:** Transform the hike into an educational experience by pointing out interesting plants, insects, or birds along the way.
- **Download Offline Maps:** Downloading a map of the levada beforehand ensures you stay on the trail, especially if traveling without internet access.
- **Leave No Trace:** Remind everyone to pack out all trash and avoid disturbing the natural environment.

The Levada das 25 Fontes offers a delightful introduction to Madeira's hiking trails and its stunning Laurissilva Forest. With its manageable distance, beautiful scenery, and enchanting waterfalls, this hike is a perfect choice for families seeking a memorable outdoor adventure on the island.

4.2 Vereda do Paul do Mar: Cliffside Adventure with Panoramic Ocean Views

The Vereda do Paul do Mar is a breathtaking cliffside hike offering stunning panoramic views of the Atlantic Ocean. This moderate-difficulty trail is a must-do for adventurous hikers seeking a challenge with rewarding scenery.

Trail Information:

- **Distance:** 6.5 kilometers (4 miles) round trip
- **Duration:** 3-4 hours
- **Difficulty:** Moderate
- **Elevation Gain:** 400 meters (1300 feet)
- **Type:** Out and back

Trail Description:

The trail kicks off in the charming village of Paul do Mar, a traditional fishing community nestled along the rugged coastline. The initial path winds through banana plantations and terraced fields, offering glimpses of the turquoise waters crashing against the volcanic rocks below. Breathe in the fresh air and savor the tranquility of the area, a stark contrast to the upcoming challenge.

As you ascend, the lush vegetation transitions to a landscape characteristic of the Laurissilva forest, a UNESCO World Heritage Site. Here, keep an eye out for the unique flora and fauna, remnants of a bygone era, like the Madeira laurel tree (Laurus nobilis) and the trocaz pigeon (Columba trocaz), a vulnerable endemic species. The trail then takes a dramatic turn, hugging the cliffs and providing a true test of your adventurous spirit.

Highlights:

- Breathtaking panoramic views of the Atlantic Ocean, stretching as far as the eye can see
- Cliffside walking with dramatic scenery that will take your breath away
- Chance to spot seabirds like Cory's shearwater (Calonectris borealis) and marine life like dolphins playing in the waves below
- Tranquil atmosphere away from the crowds, offering a chance to reconnect with nature

Tips:

- Wear sturdy hiking boots with good grip for uneven and potentially slippery terrain.
- Bring plenty of water, especially during hot weather, as there are limited options to refill along the trail.
- Pack sunscreen and a hat for sun protection, as well as sunglasses to shield your eyes from the glare reflecting off the ocean.
- Be aware of potential strong winds, especially near cliff edges. Take extra caution and avoid venturing too close during windy conditions.
- The trail can be slippery after rain, so proceed with caution and be mindful of your footing.

Additional Information:

- There are several viewpoints along the trail where you can stop, take a breather, and truly soak in the scenery. Don't forget your camera to capture these unforgettable moments.
- The trail can be combined with a visit to the natural pools

47

(piscinas naturais) in Paul do Mar for a refreshing swim after your hike. The perfect way to cool down and relax after conquering the challenging مسیر (masīr, Arabic for "path") or trail.

- Local guides are available for hire if you prefer a guided hiking experience. They can provide valuable insights into the local flora and fauna, as well as the history and culture of Madeira.

Remember:

- Leave no trace and respect the natural environment by packing out all your trash.
- Be aware of your surroundings and stay on the marked trail to avoid getting lost or injuring yourself.
- Hike at your own pace and take breaks when needed. Listen to your body and don't be afraid to turn back if you feel uncomfortable.

Enjoy the Vereda do Paul do Mar and its unforgettable cliffside adventure!

4.3 Caldeirão Verde: Hiking Through the Enchanted Laurissilva Forest (UNESCO World Heritage Site)

The Levada do Caldeirão Verde is one of Madeira's most popular hikes, and for good reason. This moderate trail winds through the heart of the Laurissilva Forest, a UNESCO World Heritage Site teeming with ancient trees, lush vegetation, and cascading waterfalls. Here's your guide to hiking Levada do Caldeirão Verde in 2024:

Trail (gaiyou, overview) and Difficulty

- Distance: 13 kilometers (8 miles) round trip
- Time: 4-6 hours to complete
- Difficulty: Moderate. The trail is mostly flat, but its length requires good stamina. There are also some uneven sections and four unlit tunnels.

What to Expect

- **Enchanted Laurissilva Forest:** Immerse yourself in the fairytale-like Laurisilva Forest, a relic from the Tertiary era. Walk along the levada (irrigation channel) surrounded by towering trees, ferns, and vibrant flowers.
- **Caldeirão Verde Waterfall:** The hike culminates at the Caldeirão Verde waterfall, a cascading gem that plunges into a beautiful emerald lagoon.
- **Levada Walk:** Enjoy the unique levada system, a network of channels that channel water throughout Madeira's mountainous terrain.

Preparation

- **Wear proper footwear:** Hiking boots or sturdy shoes with good grip are essential for the uneven terrain.
- **Pack weatherproof clothing:** Madeira's weather can be unpredictable. Bring rain gear, a hat, and sunscreen.
- **Bring plenty of water and snacks:** Stay hydrated and fueled throughout the hike.
- **Headlamp or torch:** You'll need a light source for the unlit tunnels.

49

- **Consider a guided tour:** Guided hikes can offer insights into the local flora and fauna, and ensure safety on the trail.

Additional Tips

- **Start early:** The trail can get crowded, especially during peak season. Starting your hike early will allow you to enjoy the scenery at a quieter pace.
- **Respect the environment:** The Laurissilva Forest is a delicate ecosystem. Stick to the trail, avoid littering, and be mindful of the plants and wildlife.

Enjoying the Magic of Caldeirão Verde

With its stunning scenery, rich history, and moderate challenge, the Levada do Caldeirão Verde is a must-do for hikers visiting Madeira. So lace up your boots, grab your camera, and get ready to be enchanted by the beauty of this unforgettable trail.

5

Central Madeira - Mountain Peaks, Vineyards, and Picturesque Villages

Central Madeira unfolds like a breathtaking tapestry, offering a captivating blend of nature's majesty, historical intrigue, and local charm. Hikers will find themselves in paradise, traversing dramatic mountain peaks that pierce the clouds, lush valleys brimming with life, and a network of levadas (irrigation channels) that snake through the verdant landscape.

Standing tall amongst these peaks is Pico Ruivo, Madeira's crown jewel, reaching a staggering 1,862 meters (6,109 ft). On a clear day, the reward for your ascent is a glimpse of the neighboring island of Porto Santo, shimmering on the horizon. But Pico Ruivo isn't alone. Pico do Arieiro (1,818 meters or 5,966 ft) and Pico das Torres (1,850 meters or 6,070 ft) stand shoulder-to-shoulder, each offering panoramic vistas that will leave you breathless.

Venture beyond the mountain peaks and discover the heart of Madeira's rich viticulture. The volcanic soils of the island provide the perfect foundation for flourishing grapevines, and a long tradition of winemaking imbues the region with a unique character. Here, you can delve into the world of Madeira wine, a fortified wine matured in hot, stuffy conditions that lends it a complex and distinctive flavor profile. Dotted throughout central Madeira are numerous vineyards, welcoming visitors to learn about the meticulous winemaking process and indulge in tastings of these local treasures.

Adding a touch of fairytale charm to the landscape are the picturesque villages that nestle amidst the mountains and valleys. Santana, a haven for tourists, boasts traditional thatched-roof houses that resemble little gingerbread dwellings. History whispers from the cobbled streets of Curral das Freiras, a mountain village that served as a refuge for nuns fleeing pirate attacks. And for a glimpse into Madeira's past, Machico stands as the island's oldest settlement, offering a fascinating journey through time.

Central Madeira is more than just a collection of sights; it's an experience that lingers long after your visit. From the heart-pounding hikes to the delectable wines and the captivating villages, this region promises a unique blend of adventure, relaxation, and cultural immersion. So, lace up your hiking boots, raise a glass to local traditions, and get ready to discover the magic that awaits in central Madeira.

5.1 Balcões Viewpoint: A Short Hike with Breathtaking Views of Ribeira Brava Valley

Not every hike needs to be an epic, muscle-burning trek. Sometimes, the most rewarding journeys come in delightfully short packages. The Balcões Viewpoint near Ribeiro Frio village exemplifies this perfectly. This easy levada walk, clocking in at a manageable 1.5 kilometers (1 mile), rewards you with absolutely breathtaking panoramas of the Ribeira Brava Valley.

A Gentle Stroll Through a Verdant Paradise

The beauty of the Balcões Viewpoint hike lies in its accessibility. Unlike some of Madeira's more challenging trails, this path is ideal for families with young children, casual walkers, or anyone seeking a relaxed introduction to the island's unique levada network. The Levada do Balcões, the irrigation channel you'll be following, winds its way through the heart of the Laurissilva Forest, a UNESCO World Heritage Site. Imagine yourself strolling along a mostly flat, well-maintained trail, enveloped by towering trees, vibrant flowers, and the gentle murmur of the levada water – a symphony of nature that instantly soothes the soul. Sure, there might be occasional muddy patches, especially after rainfall, so sturdy shoes are your best bet. But the easy incline and manageable distance ensure a comfortable walk for all.

A Breathtaking Revelation: The Unveiling of the Ribeira Brava Valley

As you continue your leisurely stroll, keep your eyes peeled. The true magic unfolds as you reach the Balcões Viewpoint. Here, the landscape dramatically transforms before your very eyes. The verdant embrace of the Laurissilva Forest gives way to a breathtaking panorama of the Ribeira Brava Valley. Rolling

Conquering Pico do Arieiro requires careful planning and preparation. Here's what you need to know:

- **Gear Up:** Sturdy hiking boots with good ankle support are essential. Pack weatherproof clothing, including layers you can adjust to the changing temperatures. Don't forget sunscreen, a hat, sunglasses, and plenty of water. Hiking poles can also be helpful for providing stability on the uneven terrain.
- **Know the Conditions:** Madeira's weather can be unpredictable. Check the forecast before you set off and be prepared for anything, from sunshine to strong winds and fog. It's always better to be safe than sorry.
- **Fuel Your Adventure:** Pack enough high-energy snacks and water to keep you fueled throughout the hike. Reaching the summit requires sustained effort, so staying hydrated and nourished is crucial.
- **Consider a Guide:** While experienced hikers can tackle Pico do Arieiro independently, a guided hike can offer valuable insights into the local flora and fauna, as well as ensure your safety on the trail, especially during challenging weather conditions.

A Hike for the Determined

The Pico do Arieiro hike is a challenging yet rewarding experience. It's a test of your physical and mental strength, but the sense of accomplishment at the summit is unparalleled. As you stand on the peak, gazing out at the breathtaking views, you'll understand why this hike is a must-do for any adventurous traveler visiting Madeira.

Additional Tips

- **Start Early:** Especially during peak season, the trail can get crowded. Starting your hike early allows you to avoid the crowds and enjoy the sunrise from the summit – a truly magical experience.
- **Respect the Environment:** Leave no trace behind. Stick to the designated trail, dispose of your waste properly, and help preserve the natural beauty of this iconic mountain.

Are You Ready for the Challenge?

Pico do Arieiro awaits those who seek a thrilling adventure. So, if you're an experienced hiker looking to push your limits and experience the majesty of Madeira, this challenging yet rewarding hike is for you. With careful planning, the right gear, and a determined spirit, you can conquer Pico do Arieiro and add this unforgettable achievement to your travel log.

5.3 Queimadas Forest: Hiking Amongst Vineyards and Traditional Villages

Beyond the dramatic peaks and well-known levadas, Madeira offers hidden gems waiting to be explored. The Queimadas Forest carves a unique path through the island's heart, weaving together vineyards, charming villages, and pockets of native forest – a haven for hikers seeking a taste of Madeira's diverse landscapes and rich traditions.

A Tapestry of Landscapes

The Queimadas Forest hike unfolds like a captivating tapestry. Unlike the mountainous levada walks, this trail winds through rolling hills adorned with vineyards, the lifeblood of Madeira's renowned wine industry. Imagine yourself surrounded by emerald green vines, their leaves glistening in the sunlight.

As you walk, the intoxicating aroma of grapes may fill the air, hinting at the island's delicious wines that await you later.

The trail weaves seamlessly between these vineyards and pockets of indigenous forest. Here, towering trees cast dappled shadows, offering a cool respite on a warm day. Listen closely, and you might hear the melodious calls of native birds flitting through the branches. This unexpected encounter with nature adds a touch of wilderness to the cultivated landscape.

A Journey Through Time: Encountering Traditional Villages

Dotted along the Queimadas Forest hike are charming villages, each with its own story to tell. Step back in time as you wander through cobbled streets lined with traditional houses, their colorful facades adding a vibrant touch to the scenery. Engage with the friendly locals, who may even offer you a taste of the island's homemade delicacies or share fascinating stories about Madeira's rich history and culture.

A Hike Tailored for All

The beauty of the Queimadas Forest hike lies in its accessibility. The trails are generally well-maintained and offer a moderate level of difficulty, making them suitable for hikers of varying experience levels. Whether you're a seasoned adventurer or a casual walker seeking a scenic stroll, this trail caters to all.

Planning Your Madeira Adventure

- **Comfortable Footwear:** Sturdy shoes with good grip are recommended, as the terrain can vary from paved paths to uneven forest trails.
- **Sun Protection:** Madeira's sun can be strong, so pack sunscreen, a hat, and sunglasses.
- **Hydration and Snacks:** Bring plenty of water and snacks to keep you fueled throughout your hike. Some villages may

have small cafes where you can refresh yourself.

Making the Most of Your Experience

- **Explore the Villages:** Don't just pass through the villages – take some time to explore their hidden corners, interact with the locals, and soak up the authentic Madeiran atmosphere.
- **Sample the Local Wines:** After your hike, indulge in a tasting of Madeira's world-famous wines. Many vineyards in the area offer tours and tastings, allowing you to experience the island's rich winemaking tradition firsthand.

A Hike Beyond the Expected

The Queimadas Forest hike offers more than just scenic beauty. It's a journey that blends nature, culture, and tradition, providing a glimpse into the heart of Madeira. So, lace up your shoes, grab your camera, and embark on this unique adventure. The Queimadas Forest awaits, ready to unveil its hidden treasures.

6

East Madeira - Waterfalls, Water Mills, and Secluded Beaches

East Madeira unfolds like a captivating tapestry, where rolling hills adorned with vineyards meet the rugged beauty of the Atlantic coastline. This unique landscape offers a distinct contrast to the dramatic mountains and lush forests found in the central and western parts of the island, but with its own charm and treasures to discover. Here, you'll find a delightful blend of relaxation, cultural exploration, and natural wonders, all waiting to be unveiled.

- Cascading Delights: Waterfalls and Water Mills

East Madeira boasts a network of levadas (irrigation channels) that weave through the hillsides like veins, providing not only life-giving water for the island's agriculture but also creating opportunities for scenic walks and delightful surprises. The PR 9 Levada do Caniçal is a popular choice, offering hikers a glimpse into the charming Caniçal village, a place steeped in local tradition. And what better way to end your walk than with

60

the refreshing reward of the waterfall cascading down at the levada's conclusion? Another option is the PR 11 Levada da Rocha Vermelha, which winds through a verdant valley teeming with vegetation before reaching a hidden waterfall, a perfect spot to commune with nature.

Dotted throughout the eastern landscape, you'll also find remnants of Madeira's agricultural heritage – water mills. These historical structures, some dating back centuries, stand as testaments to human ingenuity and the island's deep connection to water. Imagine stepping back in time as you explore these silent sentinels, their weathered stones whispering tales of a bygone era.

- Secluded Havens: Beaches Made for Relaxation

East Madeira boasts a string of hidden coves and secluded beaches, ideal for those seeking a tranquil escape. Imagine sinking your toes into the black sand beach of Prainha da Machico, a unique bathing experience with a dramatic backdrop of volcanic cliffs that plunge into the ocean. Or, for a more family-friendly option, the golden sands of Praia da Baixa da Machico beckon with their gentle waves and ample space for building sandcastles and soaking up the sunshine. And don't miss the natural pools of Reis Magos, perfect for a refreshing dip in the crystal-clear Atlantic waters. These sheltered pools offer a safe haven for swimming and snorkeling, surrounded by volcanic rock formations that create a sense of tranquility.

- A Journey Through Time: Charming Villages Steeped in History

East Madeira is sprinkled with traditional villages, each with its own story to tell. Santa Cruz, the easternmost town on the island, boasts a rich history dating back to the 15th century. Explore its charming harbor, a lively hubbub of colorful fishing boats bringing in their daily catch, and immerse yourself in the town's unique culture. Machico, the island's oldest settlement, offers a fascinating glimpse into Madeira's past through its historical landmarks and traditional architecture. Wander through its cobbled streets lined with colorful houses, and visit its historical sites like the Captain's House Museum, which sheds light on the island's early settlers and explorers.

Camara de Lobos, a picturesque fishing village nestled on the southern coast, is famous for its colorful boats that bob gently in the harbor. Here, you can savor the freshest seafood at one of the many waterfront restaurants, enjoying the breathtaking views as the aroma of grilled fish fills the air. As you explore these villages, don't hesitate to strike up a conversation with the friendly locals, who are known for their warm hospitality and love for sharing their island's stories.

East Madeira is a destination that caters to all. Whether you seek adventure on the levada trails, relaxation on secluded beaches, or a journey through time in charming villages, this alluring corner of Madeira promises an unforgettable experience. So, lace up your walking shoes, pack your swimsuit, and prepare to be enchanted by the magic of East Madeira.

6.1 Levada do Caniçal: Lush Forests and Refreshing Waterfalls near Machico

Craving a scenic escape amidst lush greenery and the invigorating reward of a cascading waterfall? The Levada do Caniçal near Machico offers the perfect solution. This easy-to-moderate levada walk, suitable for most fitness levels, unfolds like a verdant tapestry, leading you towards a refreshing waterfall and captivating coastal panoramas.

A Verdant Tunnel Beckons

The Levada do Caniçal walk begins near the tunnel connecting Machico and Caniçal. As you embark on your journey, the levada itself becomes your guide, gently weaving its way through a landscape brimming with life. Towering trees with vibrant green foliage create a natural canopy overhead, providing a welcome respite from the sun on warm days. Listen closely, and you might be rewarded with the melodious calls of exotic birds flitting through the branches. The air itself carries the refreshing scent of damp earth and mengalir (the water channel), creating a truly invigorating atmosphere.

A Gradual Ascent with Unveiling Vistas

The Levada do Caniçal offers a manageable climb, making it suitable for walkers of varying experience levels. The well-maintained path winds its way through the verdant hillsides, offering occasional glimpses of the sapphire-blue ocean sparkling in the distance. As you ascend, charming traditional houses nestled amidst the greenery might peek through the trees, adding a touch of human history to the natural beauty. Keep your eyes peeled for colorful bursts of bougainvillea cascading over whitewashed walls – a signature sight in Madeira.

The Cascading Finale: A Moment of Rejuvenation

After a leisurely walk, the sound of cascading water grows louder, announcing your arrival at the star attraction – the waterfall. The Levada do Caniçal culminates in a magnificent cascade, its cool waters tumbling down the rocks and collecting in a crystal-clear pool at the base. Take a moment to soak in the beauty of this natural wonder. Feel the cool mist spray your face, listen to the symphony of cascading water, and breathe in the fresh air – a truly rejuvenating experience.

Planning Your Escape to the Levada

The Levada do Caniçal is a fantastic year-round choice, but Madeira's weather can be unpredictable. Pack light rain gear and sunscreen, just in case. Bringing a reusable water bottle and a small snack is recommended, although there are cafes in Machico for refreshments before or after your hike. Sturdy shoes with good tread are essential for navigating the uneven terrain.

Making the Most of Your Machico Adventure

- **Embrace the Serenity:** The Levada do Caniçal offers a welcome escape from the hustle and bustle. Take your time, savor the tranquility of the surroundings, and disconnect from the outside world. Perhaps pack a light book to enjoy by the waterfall, or simply sit back and listen to the sounds of nature.
- **Capture the Beauty:** Don't forget your camera! The levada walk boasts an abundance of scenic opportunities, from the lush greenery and colorful flora to the cascading waterfall. You might even capture a glimpse of the local wildlife, such as rabbits scampering through the undergrowth or playful butterflies flitting between flowers.
- **Explore Machico:** After your hike, take some time to explore

the charming town of Machico. Wander through its historical center, visit the interesting museums like the Captain's
House Museum to learn about the island's early settlers,
or relax on the beach and soak up the sunshine. Sample
the fresh seafood at the harborside restaurants, and don't
forget to try a glass of Madeira wine, the island's famous
fortified beverage.

A Short Hike with Lasting Memories

The Levada do Caniçal walk may be short in distance, but
it delivers a powerful punch of natural beauty and a sense of
rejuvenation. It's the perfect way to experience the unique
levada network of Madeira and to discover a hidden gem near
Machico. So lace up your shoes, grab your camera, and get ready
to be enchanted by the cascading waters, verdant landscapes,
and the undeniable charm of the Levada do Caniçal.

6.2 PR 9 Levada da Serra do Faial: Discover Historic Water Mills and Stunning Landscapes

Journey beyond the typical tourist path and immerse yourself in
the rich history and captivating landscapes of Madeira with the
PR 9 Levada da Serra do Faial hike. This moderately challenging
route unfolds like a living tapestry, weaving together traditional
water mills, enchanting forests, and breathtaking mountain
vistas.

A Walk Through Time: Encountering Water Mills

The PR 9 Levada da Serra do Faial isn't just a scenic walk; it's
a journey through time. Scattered along the levada (irrigation
channel) are silent sentinels of Madeira's agricultural heritage
– water mills. These historical structures, some dating back

centuries, stand as testaments to human ingenuity and the island's deep connection to water. Imagine stepping back in time as you explore these weathered stone structures, their silent presence whispering tales of a bygone era.

A Feast for the Senses: Lush Forests and Scenic Vistas

As you venture deeper into the heart of the Serra do Faial (Faial Mountain Range), the landscape transforms into a verdant paradise. Towering trees with vibrant foliage create a lush canopy overhead, filtering sunlight and creating a cool, refreshing atmosphere. Listen closely and you might be rewarded with the melodic calls of birds flitting through the branches, adding a touch of life to the serene surroundings. The levada itself becomes your guide, gently meandering through the verdant hillsides. Keep your eyes peeled for occasional breaks in the trees, revealing breathtaking glimpses of the rugged coastline and the sapphire-blue expanse of the Atlantic Ocean.

A Moderate Challenge with Rewarding Vistas

The PR 9 Levada da Serra do Faial offers a moderate challenge, making it suitable for hikers with a decent level of fitness. The well-maintained path features some inclines and uneven terrain, so sturdy shoes with good grip are essential. However, the rewards are more than worth the effort. As you conquer each incline, you'll be greeted with ever-more-expansive panoramic views, allowing you to appreciate the true scale and majesty of the surrounding landscapes.

Planning Your Historical Hike

The PR 9 Levada da Serra do Faial is a fantastic option any time of year. However, Madeira's weather can be unpredictable. So, it's always wise to pack light rain gear and sunscreen, just in case. A reusable water bottle and snacks are recommended to keep you fueled throughout your hike. While there aren't refreshment stands along the trail, there are cafes in some of the villages you might pass through before or after your hike.

Enhancing Your Experience

- **Explore the Villages:** The trail may lead you through charming villages. Take a moment to wander through their cobbled streets, admire the traditional architecture, and perhaps engage with the friendly locals who are known for their warm hospitality. You might even stumble upon a local market or a hidden gem like a small family-run restaurant serving delicious Madeiran cuisine.
- **Learn About the Water Mills:** Research the history of the water mills before your hike. Understanding their function and significance will add another layer of appreciation as you encounter them along the way. Imagine the bustling activity that once surrounded these structures, and the vital role they played in the island's agricultural development.

A Hike Beyond the Expected

The PR 9 Levada da Serra do Faial hike offers more than just scenic beauty. It's a captivating blend of history, nature, and culture, providing a glimpse into the heart of Madeira. So, lace up your shoes, grab your camera, and embark on this extraordinary journey. The PR 9 Levada da Serra do Faial awaits, ready to unveil its hidden treasures and leave you with memories that will linger long after your visit.

6.3 Ponta de São Lourenço Nature Reserve: Hiking on a Volcanic Peninsula with Dramatic Coastlines

Calling all nature enthusiasts and hiking aficionados! The Ponta de São Lourenço Nature Reserve beckons, offering a unique hiking experience on Madeira's easternmost tip. This dramatic peninsula, sculpted by volcanic eruptions and relentless Atlantic winds, promises stunning coastal vistas, otherworldly landscapes, and a chance to immerse yourself in a protected haven teeming with diverse flora and fauna.

A Landscape Shaped by Fire and Wind

The Ponta de São Lourenço Nature Reserve is a geologist's paradise. Volcanic activity millions of years ago laid the foundation for this dramatic landscape. As you hike, you'll encounter jagged black lava rock formations sculpted by time and the relentless Atlantic winds. Imagine traversing a lunar-like terrain, with fiery oranges, deep reds, and inky blacks dominating the color palette. These volcanic fingerprints paint a picture of Madeira's fiery past.

A Biodiversity Haven: A Celebration of Nature

Despite the seemingly barren volcanic landscape, the Ponta de São Lourenço Nature Reserve thrives with life. Look closely, and you'll discover a surprising variety of flora adapted to the harsh conditions. Endemic flowers in vibrant hues peek out from crevices, while low-lying shrubs tenaciously cling to the rocky slopes. Keep an eye out for Madeira's endemic birds soaring overhead, their calls echoing through the vastness of the reserve. This sanctuary provides a vital habitat for these feathered residents, making your hike a chance to witness the beauty of nature's resilience.

A Hike Tailored for All

The beauty of the Ponta de São Lourenço Nature Reserve lies in its accessibility. The main hiking trail, the Vereda da Ponta de São Lourenço (PR8), is a moderately challenging route offering rewarding payoffs. The well-maintained path winds its way along the peninsula, providing ample opportunities to capture breathtaking panoramas of the rugged coastline and the endless expanse of the Atlantic Ocean. For those seeking a shorter option, there's also the trail leading to the Casa do Sardinha, a small bar offering refreshments with a million-dollar view.

Planning Your Volcanic Voyage

- **Gear Up for the Elements:** Madeira's weather can be unpredictable. Pack sunscreen, sunglasses, and a hat for sun protection. Light rain gear is also recommended, especially during the winter months. Sturdy shoes with good tread are essential for navigating the rocky terrain.
- **Bring Essentials:** Pack a reusable water bottle and snacks to keep you fueled throughout your hike. While there are no restaurants along the main trail, there are cafes near the starting point at Baía d'Abra.
- **Respect the Environment:** The Ponta de São Lourenço Nature Reserve is a protected area. Stay on designated trails, avoid littering, and leave no trace behind. Help preserve this unique ecosystem for future generations to enjoy.

An Unforgettable Adventure Awaits

The Ponta de São Lourenço Nature Reserve offers a hiking experience unlike any other in Madeira. It's a chance to explore a volcanic wonderland, witness the power of nature, and appreciate the island's unique biodiversity. So lace up your shoes, grab your camera, and get ready to embark on an unforgettable adventure. The dramatic landscapes, diverse flora and fauna, and breathtaking coastal vistas of the Ponta de São Lourenço Nature Reserve await!

III

Beyond the Trails: Enriching Your Madeira Experience

7

Unveiling Madeira's Culture and History: Museums, Local Cuisine, and Traditions

Madeira, a Portuguese archipelago nestled in the Atlantic Ocean, boasts a rich tapestry of culture and history. Volcanic eruptions millions of years ago birthed this scenic island, later discovered and colonized by the Portuguese in the 15th century. Madeira's identity is a fascinating blend of European influence and island ingenuity, reflected in its museums, delectable cuisine, and time-honored traditions.

Unveiling the Past: Madeira's Museums

- **Monte Palace Tropical Garden:** This sprawling estate offers more than just a glimpse into Madeira's exotic flora. The palace itself, built in the early 18th century, showcases a fascinating collection of azulejo tiles, a form of Portuguese painted ceramic art. Visitors can wander through themed gardens boasting plants from five continents, or take a scenic cable car ride for breathtaking panoramic views.
- **CR7 Museum:** For football (soccer) fans, a visit to the CR7 Museum is a must. Dedicated to Madeira's most famous son,

Cristiano Ronaldo, the museum chronicles his incredible career journey through trophies, interactive exhibits, and holographic displays. Even non-football enthusiasts will appreciate the dedication and hard work that propelled Ronaldo to become one of the greatest players in the world.

· **Santa Clara Municipal Museum:** Delve deeper into Madeira's historical and cultural heritage at the Santa Clara Municipal Museum. Housed in a former convent built in the 15th century, the museum's collection spans religious art, archaeological artifacts, and exhibits showcasing the island's traditional crafts and industries like embroidery and winemaking.

A Culinary Journey: Local Cuisine of Madeira

Madeira's cuisine is a delightful fusion of Portuguese flavors with fresh, locally-sourced ingredients. Fresh seafood features prominently, with dishes like "Espadarte e Banana" (scabbard fish with banana) and "Lapas" (limpets) being local favorites. Venture beyond the coast and sample "Carne de Vinha d'Alhos" (garlic and wine marinated beef) or "Estruvadinho" (stewed rabbit), both staples of Madeiran cuisine. Don't miss "Bolo do Caco" (sweet potato bread) and "Espremada" (garlic sausage skewers) for a taste of Madeiran comfort food. And to end your meal on a high note, indulge in a glass of Madeira wine, the island's renowned fortified wine. Madeira wine comes in a variety of styles, from dry to sweet, each boasting a complex flavor profile influenced by the unique volcanic soil and aging process.

Keeping Traditions Alive

Madeira's vibrant festivals and traditions are a captivating way to experience the island's soul. The **Madeira Wine Festival,** held annually in September, is a colorful celebration overflowing with grape-treading ceremonies, parades filled with costumed dancers, and lively music performances. During Christmas, the island transforms into a winter wonderland, illuminated by dazzling lights and festive decorations. Immerse yourself in the lively **Christmas Eve church services** ("Missa do Galo") for a truly unforgettable experience. The night comes alive with the sounds of traditional instruments and carol singing, followed by a celebratory family feast. Another fascinating tradition is the **Festa dos Santos Populares** (Festival of Popular Saints) held throughout June. Madeira's streets come alive with colorful flower carpets, religious processions, and locals dressed in traditional attire. Be sure to sample the traditional foods and beverages offered during these festivities for a taste of Madeiran hospitality.

Madeira's cultural and historical offerings are as captivating as its dramatic volcanic landscapes. So, delve into its museums, savor its delectable cuisine, and immerse yourself in its time-honored traditions for an unforgettable Madeiran experience.

7.1 Must-See Museums and Cultural Sites in Funchal

Funchal, the capital of Madeira, offers a wealth of museums and cultural sites to enrich your understanding of the island's fascinating history and heritage. Here are 7 must-see options to add to your itinerary:

1. **Quinta das Cruzes Museum:** Nestled amidst lush gardens, this 18th-century mansion transformed into a museum showcases Madeira's artistic legacy. Explore its collection of decorative arts, including paintings, sculptures, furni-

75

ture, and ceramics. Admire religious art and archaeological artifacts that offer a glimpse into the island's faith and the lives of its past inhabitants.

2. **CR7 Museum:** Calling all football (soccer) fans! The CR7 Museum is a pilgrimage site dedicated to Madeira's most famous son, Cristiano Ronaldo. Delve into his incredible career journey through a collection of trophies, interactive exhibits, and holographic displays. Even if you're not a die-hard fan, the museum offers a compelling look at the dedication and hard work that propelled Ronaldo to become one of the greatest players in the world.

3. **Madeira Story Centre:** Immerse yourself in a captivating journey through Madeira's history, culture, and natural environment at the Madeira Story Centre. This unique, modern museum utilizes interactive exhibits and multimedia presentations to bring the island's story to life. Learn about Madeira's volcanic origins, explore its rich maritime heritage, and discover the traditional ways of life that have shaped the Madeiran people for generations.

4. **Santa Clara Municipal Museum:** Step back in time at the Santa Clara Municipal Museum, housed within the walls of a 15th-century convent. Explore the museum's collection, which spans religious art and archaeological artifacts. Uncover the island's cultural heritage through exhibits showcasing traditional crafts and industries like embroidery and winemaking –(dochira mo = both) essential parts of the Madeiran identity.

5. **Sé Cathedral:** History and architecture buffs won't want to miss Funchal's majestic cathedral, Sé Cathedral. Construction began in the 15th century, resulting in a stunning blend of Gothic, Manueline, and Renaissance architectural styles.

Step inside to marvel at the gilded woodwork, stained-glass windows, and religious art that adorn the interior.

6. **Monte Palace Tropical Garden:** Escape the city center and explore the sprawling Monte Palace Tropical Garden. This magnificent estate boasts more than just a vibrant collection of exotic flora from five continents. Explore the 18th-century palace itself, showcasing a fascinating collection of azulejo tiles, a form of Portuguese painted ceramic art. Don't miss the opportunity to take a scenic cable car ride and soak in breathtaking panoramic views of the surroundings.

7. **Fortaleza de São Tiago:** Standing sentinel over Funchal's harbor for centuries, Fortaleza de São Tiago is a star-shaped fortress dating back to the 17th century. Explore the ramparts, dungeons, and armory to delve into Madeira's role in Portugal's maritime defense system. The fortress also houses the Military Museum of Madeira, where you can discover weapons, uniforms, and artifacts that tell the story of the island's military history.

7.2 Savoring the Flavors of Madeira: Local Dishes and Culinary Delights

Madeira's cuisine is a delightful fusion of Portuguese flavors with fresh, locally-sourced ingredients, reflecting the island's rich history and volcanic landscape. Here's a glimpse into some must-try dishes to tantalize your taste buds:

· **Fresh Seafood:** Madeira's crystal-clear waters provide an abundance of seafood, a mainstay in the local diet. A unique Madeiran dish is **Espadarte e Banana (scabbard fish with**

banana). This may surprise some, but the sweetness of the banana perfectly complements the savory scabbard fish, creating a delightful textural contrast. Another local favorite is **Lapas (limpets)**, small sea snails typically served simply grilled or with a garlicky sauce. For a more adventurous palate, try **Gambas à la Madeirense (Madeiran-style shrimp)** cooked with garlic, chili, and local herbs.

· **Meat Dishes:** Meat lovers won't be disappointed by Madeiran cuisine. **Carne de Vinha d'Alhos (garlic and wine marinated beef)** is a succulent and flavorful dish, where the beef is marinated in garlic, wine, and spices before being grilled or fried. For a heartier option, **Estruvadinho (stewed rabbit)** is a comforting dish, traditionally slow-cooked with vegetables and white wine.

· **Comfort Food:** Madeira offers an array of comforting dishes perfect for a casual meal or a cozy evening in. **Bolo do Caco (sweet potato bread)** is a staple side dish or can be enjoyed on its own. This savory flatbread made with sweet potato flour is often served with garlic butter or cheese. **Espremada (garlic sausage skewers)** are another popular choice, featuring grilled sausage cubes skewered with garlic and bay leaves. These savory skewers are a perfect accompaniment to a glass of Madeira wine.

· **Madeira Wine:** No culinary exploration of Madeira is complete without indulging in its world-renowned fortified wine. Madeira wine boasts a complex flavor profile, ranging from dry to sweet, all influenced by the island's volcanic soil and unique aging process. During your visit, take a winery tour to learn about the winemaking process and savor different varieties, each with its own distinct character.

Beyond the Plate: Must-Try Madeiran Drinks

- **Poncha:** This refreshing local beverage is a must-try, especially on a warm day. Made with rum, lemon juice, honey, and sugar cane juice, poncha is typically served with a lemon peel. While some variations include other fruits like orange or passion fruit, the classic recipe is a true testament to Madeiran simplicity.
- **Coral Beer:** Madeira's own brewery produces Coral beer, a popular choice among locals and visitors alike. This crisp, refreshing lager pairs perfectly with many Madeiran dishes, especially seafood and grilled meats.
- **Nikita:** For a taste of something unique, try Nikita, a liqueur made from the fruit of the prickly pear cactus. This sweet liqueur can be enjoyed on its own or as a digestif after a meal.

7.3 Experiencing Traditional Festivals and Events Throughout the Year

Madeira bursts with vibrant energy throughout the year, thanks to its rich tapestry of traditional festivals and events. Here's a glimpse into some of the highlights you might encounter on your Madeiran adventure:

- **February: Carnival** - Immerse yourself in the electrifying atmosphere of Madeira's Carnival, a riot of color, music, and dance. Elaborate floats parade through the streets of Funchal, accompanied by costumed revelers in dazzling attire and pulsating rhythms. Don't miss the **Trapalhão** parade on Shrove Tuesday, known for its playful satire and lighthearted costumes that poke fun at current events and local personalities.

- **May: Flower Festival** - Witness a floral explosion during the Madeira Flower Festival, a celebration of spring's arrival. Marvel at the creation of a stunning "tapete" (carpet) made entirely of flowers along the main avenue in Funchal. This breathtaking artwork, meticulously designed by skilled artisans, depicts a different theme each year, using thousands of colorful blooms. Admire the vibrant flower displays that adorn balconies and public spaces throughout Funchal, and participate in the joyous parades filled with music, traditional costumes, and dancers.
- **June: Atlantic Festival** - Embrace the summer spirit at the Atlantic Festival, a month-long celebration brimming with cultural events. Witness awe-inspiring firework displays synchronized with music, a vibrant display of Madeira's pyrotechnic artistry that illuminates the night sky over Funchal Bay. Immerse yourself in the Madeira Music Festival, featuring a stellar lineup of local and international musicians across various genres. Explore the Regional Arts Week, a showcase of the island's rich artistic heritage, where you can admire exhibitions of traditional crafts, paintings, sculptures, and embroidery.
- **August: Folklore Festival** - Journey back in time at the Folklore Festival, a celebration of Madeira's unique folklore traditions. Folk groups from all over the island come together in a vibrant display of music, dance, and craftsmanship. Witness captivating performances featuring traditional dances like the **bailinho** and the **chocalho**, accompanied by the haunting melodies of instruments like the **brinquinho** (ukulele) and the **rajão** (friction drum). Stroll through stalls showcasing traditional Madeiran crafts, where you can

find everything from hand-embroidered linens and wicker baskets to intricate wood carvings and colorful ceramics.

· **October: Wine Festival** - Raise a glass to Madeira's world-famous wine during the Wine Festival. Witness grape-treading ceremonies, a symbolic tradition reflecting the island's long history of viticulture. Immerse yourself in lively parades featuring colorful floats depicting scenes from the grape harvest and costumed dancers celebrating the bounty of the season. Sample different varieties of Madeira wine, from dry whites to rich, flavorful tawnies, and savor the island's delectable cuisine during this joyous festival. Don't miss the opportunity to visit a historic winery and learn about the unique winemaking process that imbues Madeira wine with its complex flavor profile.

· **December: Christmas and New Year's Eve** - Experience the magic of Christmas in Madeira, a season of dazzling illuminations, festive decorations, and heartwarming traditions. Attend the lively "Missa do Galo" (Christmas Eve church services) filled with traditional music and carol singing, followed by a celebratory family feast featuring roasted suckling pig and other regional delicacies. Ring in the New Year with Madeira's spectacular firework displays, a breathtaking display of light and color illuminating the night sky across Funchal and many other towns. Madeira's New Year's Eve celebrations are known for their joyous atmosphere, with locals and visitors alike gathering to watch the fireworks and share in the revelry.

These are just a few of the many festivals and events that paint Madeira's cultural calendar throughout the year. So, whenever you choose to visit, you're sure to experience the warmth,

81

hospitality, and vibrant spirit of the Madeiran people through their cherished traditions.

8

Relaxation and Rejuvenation After Your Hikes: Spas, Botanical Gardens, and Local Crafts

Madeira offers the perfect blend of adventure and relaxation. After conquering its many hiking trails, you can soothe your tired muscles and rejuvenate your spirit at a luxurious spa, explore the beauty of its botanical gardens, or immerse yourself in the island's vibrant tradition of local crafts.

Spas:

Madeira boasts a number of world-class spas that offer a variety of treatments and therapies to help you unwind and recharge. Here are a few options to consider:

- **The Cliff Bay Spa at The Cliff Bay Resort:** Located in a stunning clifftop setting overlooking the Atlantic Ocean, The Cliff Bay Spa offers a haven of tranquility. Indulge in a signature massage using volcanic stones, or soak in the infinity pool while taking in the breathtaking views.
- **Reid's Palace Spa at Reid's Palace, A Belmond Hotel:** Ex-

perience pampering in a historic setting at Reid's Palace Spa. This luxurious spa offers a wide range of treatments, including facials, body wraps, and hydrotherapy.

· **Longevity Wellness Club at Savoy Palace:** This state-of-the-art spa offers a holistic approach to wellness. In addition to traditional spa treatments, the Longevity Wellness Club also features a hydrotherapy circuit, a saltwater pool, and a thermal suite.

Botanical Gardens:

· **Monte Palace Tropical Garden:** Escape the crowds and explore the Monte Palace Tropical Garden, a sprawling estate featuring a collection of plants from five continents. Wander through themed gardens adorned with orchids, lilies, and koi ponds, or take a cable car ride for panoramic views of Funchal.

· **Palheiro Gardens:** Located in the heart of Funchal, the Palheiro Gardens offer a tranquil oasis. Explore the beautifully landscaped gardens, featuring a variety of exotic plants, waterfalls, and lakes.

· **Botanical Garden of Madeira:** Discover Madeira's indigenous flora at the Botanical Garden of Madeira. This expansive garden showcases over 2,000 plant species, including the endemic Madeira Laurel tree (Laurus novocanariensis).

Local Crafts:

Madeira has a rich tradition of handicrafts, and there are many places where you can find unique souvenirs to remember your trip. Here are a few items to look for:

- **Embroidery:** Madeira embroidery is known for its intricate details and vibrant colors. You can find everything from tablecloths and napkins to clothing and wall hangings.
- **Wickerwork:** Madeira is famous for its wickerwork baskets, which are made from reeds and other natural materials. These baskets are both beautiful and functional, and make great gifts.
- **Ceramics:** Madeiran ceramics are known for their colorful glazes and traditional designs. You can find a variety of items, such as plates, cups, and vases.
- **Rugs:** Woven rugs are another popular Madeiran craft. These rugs are typically made from wool and feature geometric patterns.

So, after a day of exploring Madeira's many wonders, be sure to take some time to relax and rejuvenate at a spa, immerse yourself in the beauty of its botanical gardens, or browse the shops for unique local crafts. You're sure to find the perfect way to unwind and create lasting memories of your time on this unforgettable island.

8.1 Pampering Yourself at Natural Thermal Spas

While Madeira may not have naturally occurring hot springs like some other global spa destinations, it more than makes up for it with a remarkable collection of world-class spas. These havens of tranquility, strategically nestled amidst Madeira's dramatic coastlines, lush forests, and volcanic landscapes, offer the perfect way to unwind after a day of exploring the island's many wonders. Imagine this: you've conquered a challenging hike through Laurissilva forest, breathing in the crisp mountain

85

air and marveling at the ancient trees. Or perhaps you've spent a day kayaking along the rugged coastline, the spray of the ocean invigorating you as you explore hidden coves. Now, picture yourself sinking into a luxurious treatment at a spa that seamlessly blends pampering with the island's natural beauty. Sounds pretty good, doesn't it?

Here, we'll delve into some of Madeira's most exceptional spa options, each offering a unique experience to soothe your body and rejuvenate your spirit.

Clifftop Bliss at The Cliff Bay Spa: Imagine this: the warm caress of a signature massage using volcanic stones eases away tension in your muscles. As you drift into a state of complete relaxation, your gaze stretches out towards the seemingly endless expanse of the Atlantic Ocean. This isn't just a daydream; it's a reality waiting for you at The Cliff Bay Spa. Perched atop a stunning cliff overlooking Funchal, this haven of tranquility offers a truly unforgettable spa experience. After your invigorating massage, take a dip in the infinity pool, letting the breathtaking ocean views and the caress of the sea breeze further melt away stress. For those seeking an even more unique treatment, consider the "Madeiran Vineyard Wrap." This signature treatment incorporates the island's volcanic earth and indigenous grapes, leaving your skin feeling renewed and revitalized.

A Touch of History at Reid's Palace Spa: For those who appreciate a touch of history with their pampering, Reid's Palace Spa beckons. Located within the elegant walls of Reid's Palace, a historic hotel that has welcomed celebrities and dignitaries for over a century, this luxurious spa offers a comprehensive menu of treatments designed to leave you feeling restored. Highly trained therapists create a personalized wellness journey for each guest, combining facials and body wraps formulated with the finest natural ingredients to target your specific needs. Imagine indulging in a revitalizing Vitamin C facial, followed by a luxurious Cleopatra's Milk Bath, steeped in soothing donkey's milk and botanical oils. If you're feeling a bit sore after a day of exploration, a deep tissue massage using traditional Portuguese techniques will leave you feeling loose and limber. After your treatment, take a moment to wander the beautiful gardens surrounding the hotel, a tranquil oasis teeming with colorful flowers and exotic plants.

Embrace a Holistic Approach at Longevity Wellness Club: Catering to those seeking a comprehensive approach to wellness, the state-of-the-art Longevity Wellness Club at Savoy Palace goes beyond the expected spa treatments. While you'll find a complete menu of massages, facials, and body scrubs incorporating high-quality products, the real draw here is the focus on holistic wellbeing. Imagine invigorating your body with a session in the hydrotherapy circuit, featuring a series of strategically designed water experiences that improve circulation and ease muscle tension. Afterwards, float weightlessly in the saltwater pool, letting the gentle buoyancy soothe your entire body. To truly indulge, explore the thermal suite, offering a variety of heat therapy experiences proven to promote relaxation and detoxification. Saunas, steam rooms, and experience showers using contrasting water temperatures create a deeply therapeutic circuit that will leave you feeling utterly renewed.

Indulge in the Ocean's Bounty: Thalassotherapy in Madeira
For an extra dose of indulgence unique to Madeira, delve into the world of thalassotherapy. This practice harnesses the therapeutic powers of seawater and other marine elements to

create a truly immersive spa experience. Imagine enveloping your body in a seaweed wrap, rich in minerals and nutrients that nourish and revitalize your skin. Sea mud baths, known for their detoxifying properties, will leave you feeling cleansed and refreshed. Thalasso massages specifically designed to ease tension and promote deep relaxation will melt away any lingering stress. Some spas even offer unique treatments incorporating Madeira's indigenous marine flora, like massages using local seaweed varieties or invigorating body scrubs featuring sea salt harvested from the island's shores. By incorporating the ocean's natural bounty into their treatments, thalasso therapy centers in Madeira offer a unique opportunity to truly immerse yourself in the island's rejuvenating energy.

So, after a day of exploring Madeira's dramatic landscapes and charming towns, step into one of these luxurious spas and let the island's natural beauty and world-class pampering work their magic. From clifftop sanctuaries with breathtaking

8.2 Exploring Madeira's Botanical Gardens: A Paradise of Exotic Plants

Madeira's volcanic origins and subtropical climate have fostered a unique environment, making it a haven for a remarkable variety of plant life. Beyond the dramatic coastlines and lush forests, the island boasts a collection of botanical gardens that offer a chance to immerse yourself in a world of vibrant colors, captivating scents, and exotic flora. Whether you're a seasoned botanist or simply someone who appreciates the beauty of nature, Madeira's botanical gardens promise a captivating experience for all.

Monte Palace Tropical Garden: A Global Journey in One Place

Escape the crowds and enter a world of botanical wonders at the Monte Palace Tropical Garden. This sprawling estate, perched on a hillside overlooking Funchal, offers a captivating glimpse into the rich tapestry of plant life from five continents. As you wander through themed gardens, prepare to be transported across the globe. Imagine strolling beneath the shade of towering palm trees reminiscent of the Caribbean, or marveling at vibrant orchids native to Southeast Asia. The garden's Japanese garden is a serene oasis, featuring meticulously raked gravel, koi ponds teeming with colorful fish, and meticulously pruned bonsai trees. Don't miss the chance to take a cable car ride up to the Tropical Garden, offering breathtaking panoramic views of Funchal and the surrounding coastline.

Palheiro Gardens: Tranquility in the Heart of Funchal

For those seeking a peaceful escape within Funchal's city center, the Palheiro Gardens offer a tranquil haven. Step into this beautifully landscaped oasis and let the gentle murmur of water features and the sweet fragrance of blooming flowers wash away the city's bustle. Explore winding pathways lined with a kaleidoscope of colorful blooms, from vibrant hydrangeas to delicate azaleas. Waterfalls cascade into crystal-clear ponds, creating a sense of serenity that will leave you feeling rejuvenated. A network of hidden grottoes and charming bridges adds to the garden's enchanting ambiance. Keep an eye out for the resident peacocks that strut majestically through the gardens, adding a touch of whimsy to your exploration.

Botanical Garden of Madeira: A Celebration of Indigenous Flora

Delve deeper into Madeira's unique botanical heritage at the Botanical Garden of Madeira. This expansive garden, nestled on the slopes above Funchal, showcases over 2,000 plant species, a significant portion of which are endemic to the island. Imagine following winding paths lined with the iconic Madeira Laurel tree (Laurus novocanariensis), a majestic species that has thrived on the island for millennia. The Blandy Garden, named after a family instrumental in the development of Madeira's wine industry, showcases a diverse collection of indigenous flora, including heather, orchids, and tree ferns. The garden also features a dedicated section showcasing plants from the neighboring archipelagos of the Azores and the Canaries, allowing you to compare and contrast the unique botanical tapestry of the Macaronesia region.

Beyond the Gardens: Exploring Madeira's Laurissilva Forest

If the curated beauty of the botanical gardens has piqued your interest in Madeira's natural world, venture beyond their manicured landscapes and explore the heart of the island's primeval Laurissilva forest. This UNESCO World Heritage Site is a relic of the ancient Tethys Sea laurel forests, boasting a unique ecosystem teeming with plant life found nowhere else on Earth. Towering trees draped in emerald moss, a vibrant understory of ferns and wildflowers, and the sweet melody of endemic birdsong create an atmosphere of tranquility and primeval beauty. Hiking trails weave through this enchanted forest, offering a chance to truly immerse yourself in Madeira's extraordinary botanical heritage.

Madeira's botanical gardens offer a captivating glimpse into the island's unique flora, a testament to its rich volcanic past and subtropical climate. So, lace up your walking shoes, grab your camera, and get ready to be enchanted by the vibrant colors, captivating scents, and the sheer diversity of plant life that awaits you in these verdant havens.

8.3 Discovering Local Handicrafts and Souvenirs: Supporting Local Artisans

Madeira's rich history and cultural heritage are not only re-flected in its landscapes and festivals, but also in the vibrant tradition of local handicrafts. From intricate embroidery that has adorned Portuguese royalty to handwoven baskets that have served island communities for generations, Madeira's crafts offer a unique opportunity to take a piece of the island's soul home with you. Beyond the intrinsic beauty of these handcrafted treasures, by supporting local artisans, you're contributing to the preservation of this time-honored tradition and ensuring its survival for generations to come.

Embroidery: A Legacy Stitched with Passion

Madeira embroidery is a true art form, renowned for its intricate details, vibrant colors, and exquisite craftsmanship. This tradition dates back centuries, with early influences from Flemish and Moorish techniques. Imagine delicate tablecloths adorned with floral motifs, or wall hangings depicting scenes of Madeiran life, all meticulously hand-stitched by skilled arti-sans. The traditional embroidery method, known as "bordado Madeira," utilizes Madeira cotton thread, known for its fine quality and brilliant color retention. As you explore Funchal's shops and markets, you'll find a wide variety of embroidered items, from handkerchiefs and napkins to clothing and wall tapestries. Look for the "Bordado Madeira" seal of authenticity to ensure you're purchasing a genuine, high-quality piece.

Wickerwork: Woven with Utility and Beauty

Woven from reeds, willow branches, and other natural mate-rials, Madeira's wickerwork baskets are a testament to both functionality and beauty. These handcrafted baskets have

91

been an essential part of Madeiran life for centuries, used for everything from carrying groceries to harvesting crops. The traditional techniques have been passed down through generations, ensuring the baskets' durability and timeless design. Today, you'll find wicker baskets in all shapes and sizes, from small, delicate trinket holders to large, sturdy market baskets. Consider purchasing a basket as a practical souvenir that will not only remind you of your trip but will also be a useful addition to your home. Look for baskets with intricate woven patterns or pops of color for a unique touch.

Ceramics: A Splash of Color and Tradition

Madeira's volcanic soil and rich artistic heritage have given rise to a beautiful tradition of ceramics. Local artisans handcraft a variety of ceramic items, each imbued with the island's unique character. Imagine plates and cups adorned with colorful geometric patterns or glazed vases showcasing vibrant floral motifs. These ceramics are not just decorative; they're also quite functional, perfect for everyday use or special occasions. Exploring workshops and shops throughout Madeira, you'll find an array of ceramic pieces, some featuring traditional designs passed down through generations, while others showcase contemporary artistic interpretations. Consider purchasing a piece that reflects your personal style, or choose a set as a thoughtful gift for loved ones back home.

Rugs: Woven Stories Underfoot

Woven rugs are another cherished form of Madeiran handicraft. Traditionally made from wool, these rugs feature bold geometric patterns and vibrant colors that reflect the island's rich heritage. Imagine a handwoven rug adding a touch of warmth and character to your living room, or a smaller rug gracing the entrance of your home. The intricate patterns often tell stories or represent symbols significant to Madeiran culture. While some rugs feature traditional designs, you'll also find contemporary variations that incorporate modern sensibilities. Purchasing a woven rug is a wonderful way to add a touch of Madeiran artistry and tradition to your home decor.

Beyond the Souvenirs: Witnessing the Craft

To gain a deeper appreciation for Madeira's handicrafts, consider visiting workshops where you can witness the artisans at work. Watching their skilled hands transform raw materials into beautiful objects is a captivating experience. Many workshops offer demonstrations, allowing you to see the embroidery techniques up close or to observe the process of shaping clay into ceramic masterpieces. Some workshops even allow visitors to try their hand at a simple craft activity, a fun way to connect with the island's artistic heritage on a personal level.

By choosing locally made souvenirs and exploring the world of Madeiran handicrafts, you're not just bringing home beautiful keepsakes; you're supporting the talented artisans who keep this time-honored tradition alive. So, on your next visit to Madeira, take some time to explore the island's craft scene, appreciate the skill and dedication of local artisans, and discover a unique piece of Madeira to treasure for years to come.

9

Sustainable Hiking Practices: Protecting Madeira's Natural Beauty

Madeira's dramatic landscapes, from sky-piercing mountains to lush forests, offer a hiker's paradise. But with great trails come great responsibility. As you embark on your hiking adventures, it's important to be mindful of your impact on the island's fragile ecosystem. By adopting sustainable hiking practices, you can help ensure that Madeira's natural beauty is preserved for generations to come.

Leave No Trace: This golden rule of outdoor recreation applies here as well. Pack out all trash, including food scraps, wrappers, and tissues. There may not always be trash bins on the trails, so plan accordingly and bring a reusable bag to carry your waste until you find a proper disposal site. Avoid using single-use plastics, such as water bottles, and opt for a reusable water bottle you can refill throughout the day.

Stay on Designated Trails: Sticking to marked trails helps minimize your impact on the island's vegetation and wildlife. Venturing off the path can damage delicate plant life and disrupt animal habitats. Marked trails are also generally well-maintained and offer better footing, reducing the risk of erosion and injuries.

Respect Local Flora and Fauna: Madeira is home to a unique variety of plant and animal life, many of which are endemic to the island. Resist the urge to pick flowers or disturb wildlife. Admire the beauty of the natural world from a distance and avoid anything that could disrupt their delicate balance.

Minimize Campfire Impact: If you plan on camping, use designated fire pits and only burn seasoned firewood. Never collect firewood from the surrounding areas, as this can contribute to deforestation. Extinguish your fire completely before leaving to prevent wildfires.

Be Water Wise: Madeira's water resources are precious. While exploring the trails, be mindful of your water consumption. Bring a reusable water bottle and refill it whenever possible. Avoid using disposable wipes or excessive amounts of hand sanitizer, opting for natural alternatives like soap and water when available at designated rest areas.

Respect Local Communities: Hiking trails often traverse through farmland and rural communities. Be courteous to local residents and their property. Close gates behind you if you pass through them, and avoid making excessive noise that could disturb the tranquility of the area.

Support Sustainable Businesses: Choose accommodation and activity providers that prioritize sustainability. Look for eco-friendly certifications and businesses that support local communities and conservation efforts. By making conscious choices, you can contribute to a more sustainable tourism industry in Madeira.

Spread Awareness: Educate yourself about the island's unique ecosystem and share your knowledge with fellow hikers. Encourage others to adopt sustainable practices and leave no trace on the trails. Together, we can ensure that Madeira's natural beauty thrives for generations to come.

Hiking in Madeira is a truly rewarding experience. By following these sustainable practices, you can minimize your environmental impact and ensure that the island's breathtaking landscapes continue to inspire awe and wonder for years to come. Remember, we are all guests in this natural paradise, and it's our collective responsibility to tread lightly and leave it as pristine as we found it.

9.1 Minimizing Waste on the Trails: Responsible Disposal and Eco-Friendly Practices

Madeira's hiking trails offer a chance to immerse yourself in breathtaking scenery, from soaring mountain peaks to verdant forests. But with every adventure comes a responsibility to tread lightly and minimize your impact on the island's delicate ecosystem. Here's how you can become a champion for sustainable hiking by adopting responsible waste disposal practices and eco-friendly habits:

Plan Ahead for Zero Waste:

- **Embrace Reusable Gear:** Invest in a reusable water bottle and ditch single-use plastic bottles. Many trails offer refill stations, so you can stay hydrated without generating waste. Pack reusable containers for your snacks and lunches, opting for options that minimize packaging.
- **Plan Your Meals Wisely:** Choose snacks and lunches that come in minimal or recyclable packaging. Avoid individually wrapped items and bulkier packaging altogether. Fruits

with peels or rinds can be a great zero-waste option, and for sandwiches, reusable beeswax wraps or cloth napkins are fantastic alternatives to plastic wrap.

· **The "Pack It In, Pack It Out" Mantra:** This golden rule is the cornerstone of responsible hiking. Everything you bring onto the trail, including food scraps, wrappers, tissues, and even toilet paper, must leave the trail with you. Pack a small, reusable bag specifically for your waste and ensure it's properly disposed of at designated trash bins once you reach a trailhead or rest area.

Think Beyond Convenience:

· **Ditch the Disposable Wipes:** Wet wipes are a source of convenience, but they're not eco-friendly. Opt for a small, lightweight hand towel and a refillable bottle of natural hand sanitizer for on-the-go cleaning. Look for biodegradable hand sanitizer options to further minimize your impact.

· **Hygiene and Waste Minimization:** For longer hikes that require bathroom breaks, consider a reusable camping trowel and biodegradable waste bags. Always dispose of waste in designated areas or by burying it at least 20 cm deep and at least 60 meters away from water sources and trails.

· **Embrace Multipurpose Products:** Look for multifunctional products that can replace several single-use items. Sunscreen sticks eliminate the need for bulky bottles, and a bandana can serve as a sweat rag, napkin, or makeshift first-aid bandage.

Minimize Food Waste:

- **Plan Your Portions:** Avoid packing more food than you can comfortably eat. Not only will this lighten your load, but it will also prevent food waste. If you're unsure about portion sizes, pack a bit less and always have the option to grab a snack at a local cafe or store near the trailhead.
- **Choose Long-lasting Snacks:** Opt for snacks with a longer shelf life that won't spoil easily during your hike. Nuts, dried fruits, and granola bars are all great options.
- **Embrace Reusable Food Wraps:** Ditch cling film and aluminum foil. Invest in reusable beeswax wraps or silicone food containers to keep your food fresh and prevent spills within your backpack.

By adopting these simple practices, you can significantly reduce the amount of waste you generate on your Madeira hikes. Remember, every little bit counts! Madeira's pristine beauty thrives on responsible tourism, and by making conscious choices, you can ensure a more sustainable future for the island's breathtaking landscapes.

9.2 Respecting Wildlife and Local Flora: Leave No Trace Principles

Whenever you are in an outdoor space, you are entering the natural habitat of many wild animals and plants. Madeira, with its unique ecosystems and endemic species, is especially deserving of our respect and care. As you explore the island's hiking trails, adhering to Leave No Trace principles ensures you minimize your impact on the environment and allows wildlife and flora to flourish.

Observe from a Distance:

- **Minimize Disruption:** Avoid loud noises or sudden movements that could startle wildlife. Maintain a safe distance from animals, especially if they appear agitated or are with their young. Use binoculars or a telephoto lens for a closer look without disturbing their natural behavior.
- **Respect Animal Homes:** Steer clear of nests, dens, or burrows. These are crucial sanctuaries for animals to raise their young or seek shelter. If you encounter wildlife on the trail, give them ample space to pass and avoid blocking their path.

Leave No Trace of Your Presence:

- **Minimize Food Scraps:** Food scraps can attract unwanted animals, potentially altering their natural feeding habits and increasing the risk of human-wildlife conflicts. Store your food securely in your backpack and dispose of any scraps properly in designated bins at trailheads or rest areas.
- **Avoid Introducing New Plants:** Never plant or leave behind any seeds or foreign plant material. These can disrupt the delicate balance of the ecosystem and introduce invasive species that could harm native flora.
- **Minimize Scent:** Strong perfumes, deodorants, or lotions can linger in the air and potentially disrupt animal behavior. Opt for scent-free or natural alternatives whenever possible.

Become an Advocate for Conservation:

- **Support Local Conservation Efforts:** Research and consider supporting organizations dedicated to preserving Madeira's natural heritage.

- **Spread Awareness:** Educate yourself and others about the island's unique flora and fauna. Share your knowledge with fellow hikers and encourage them to adopt sustainable practices.
- **Report any Issues:** If you encounter any wildlife in distress, damaged habitats, or invasive plant species, report them to park authorities or relevant conservation organizations.

By following these Leave No Trace principles, you become a responsible steward of Madeira's natural wonders. Your mindful actions ensure that the island's breathtaking landscapes, diverse wildlife, and unique flora continue to thrive for generations to come. Remember, responsible hiking isn't just about enjoying the beauty of nature; it's also about preserving it for all to experience.

9.3 Supporting Sustainable Tourism Initiatives in Madeira

Madeira's natural beauty, from its dramatic coastlines to its lush forests, has long been a magnet for travelers. However, with tourism comes a responsibility to ensure this beauty is preserved for future generations. The good news is that there are many ways you, as a visitor, can actively support sustainable tourism initiatives in Madeira and minimize your environmental footprint.

Making Eco-Conscious Choices:

- **Choose Eco-Friendly Accommodations:** Look for hotels or lodges with certifications for sustainable practices. These establishments prioritize energy efficiency, water conservation, and waste reduction. Eco-lodges often incorporate local materials in their construction and integrate seamlessly into the surrounding environment.

- **Support Local Businesses:** Opt for restaurants that source local ingredients and employ local staff. This not only reduces the island's carbon footprint by minimizing transportation requirements but also injects your tourist dollars directly into the local economy. Visit farmers markets and shops run by Madeiran artisans to find unique souvenirs and support local livelihoods.
- **Participate in Responsible Tours:** Choose tour operators committed to minimizing environmental impact. Look for tours that utilize eco-friendly transportation, such as electric vehicles or bikes, and prioritize responsible wildlife watching practices. Tours that educate visitors about the island's ecology and culture not only enhance your experience but also foster a sense of appreciation for the destination.

Respecting Local Customs and Traditions:

- **Dress Modestly:** When visiting religious sites or rural areas, dress modestly to respect local customs and traditions. Opt for clothing that covers your shoulders and knees.
- **Be Mindful of Noise Levels:** Excessive noise can disrupt the tranquility of the island, especially in natural areas. Be mindful of your volume levels and avoid loud music or shouting, particularly near residential areas or wildlife habitats.
- **Reduce Resource Consumption:** Conserve water and electricity during your stay. Reuse towels and linens whenever

possible, and take shorter showers. Turn off lights and electronics when not in use. Simple actions can make a big difference.

Spreading Awareness and Advocacy:

- **Educate Yourself:** Learn about Madeira's unique ecosystems and ongoing conservation efforts. The more you know, the more you can appreciate the island's natural wonders and contribute to their preservation.
- **Reduce Souvenirs:** Instead of accumulating a large number of small trinkets, consider purchasing a few, high-quality, locally-made souvenirs that you'll treasure for years to come. This not only minimizes waste but also supports Madeiran artisans.
- **Leave No Trace:** Always adhere to Leave No Trace principles on the trails and in public spaces. Pack out all your trash, avoid disturbing wildlife, and minimize your impact on the natural environment.

By making these choices, you become an ambassador for sustainable tourism in Madeira. Your responsible actions inspire others to follow suit and contribute to a future where visitors and locals alike can enjoy the island's beauty for generations to come. Remember, sustainable travel isn't just a trend; it's a necessity for preserving the places we love to explore.

10

Bonus

Maps of Madeira's Hiking Regions and Key Trails

Madeira's Hiking Regions:

Madeira offers a diverse range of hiking trails suitable for all skill levels, from leisurely strolls along the coast to challenging ascents into the mountains. The island can be broadly divided into three main hiking regions, each boasting unique landscapes and unforgettable experiences:

- **The South Coast:** The south coast is home to some of Madeira's most popular tourist resorts, including Funchal, Caniço, and Calheta. The region offers a good mix of easy and moderate trails, perfect for those seeking a relaxed introduction to Madeira's hiking scene. Explore the charming village of Camara de Lobos, famed for its colorful fishing boats, or follow the well-maintained trails along the dramatic cliffs of Cabo Girão, Europe's highest sea cliff. Don't miss the Levada Nova trail, a gentle levada walk that winds through verdant forests and offers stunning ocean vistas.

· **The West Coast:** The west coast is known for its dramatic cliffs, secluded beaches, and verdant forests. This region caters to more experienced hikers with a taste for adventure. Hike the Vereda do Achadas da Cruz, a challenging yet rewarding trail that descends through tunnels and valleys to a secluded beach. For breathtaking ocean views and a chance to spot dolphins and whales, tackle the Ponta do Pargo Lighthouse trail, which leads to a historic lighthouse perched on a rugged clifftop. The west coast also boasts some of Madeira's most scenic levada walks, such as the Levada do Paul da Serra, which winds through a laurel forest teeming with endemic flora.

· **The Eastern Interior:** The eastern interior is home to Madeira's highest peaks, including Pico Ruivo, the island's highest point. This region offers challenging hikes through dramatic landscapes for seasoned hikers. Hike the Vereda do Pico Ruivo, a tough but incredibly rewarding trail that ascends to the island's rooftop, offering panoramic views that encompass the entire island on a clear day. Explore the Laurissilva forest, a UNESCO World Heritage Site, on the Balcónes trail, a moderately difficult route that rewards you with breathtaking mountain vistas and unique plant life. The eastern interior also boasts a network of levada walks, such as the Levada do Risco, which winds its way through valleys and offers a glimpse into the island's traditional irrigation system.

Key Hiking Trails in Madeira:

Here's a selection of some of Madeira's most popular and

rewarding hiking trails, catering to different difficulty levels
and interests:

- **Levada das 25 Fontes (Levada of the 25 Fountains):** (Moderate difficulty) This classic trail in the west of Madeira offers stunning levada scenery, with countless waterfalls cascading down moss-covered rocks and lush vegetation blanketing the مسیر (masīr) (path).
- **Vereda do Pico Ruivo (Pico Ruivo Trail):** (Challenging difficulty) This hike to the highest peak in Madeira is a must-do for experienced hikers. The trail offers breathtaking panoramic views of the entire island on a clear day, but be aware of potential weather hazards and ensure you're properly equipped before attempting this challenging ascent.
- **Balcões (Balconies):** (Moderate difficulty) This trail along the west coast offers stunning ocean views, dramatic cliffs, and unique rock formations. The balcony-like viewpoints provide unforgettable vistas, making this a popular choice for photographers and nature enthusiasts.
- **Levada do Caldeirão Verde (Levada of the Green Cauldron):** (Moderate difficulty) This moderately difficult trail winds through a beautiful laurel forest in the west of Madeira. Keep an eye out for endemic flora and cascading waterfalls as you navigate this lush and verdant levada walk.
- **Ponta de São Lourenço:** (Easy difficulty) This easy trail on the eastern tip of Madeira offers a completely different hiking experience. Explore otherworldly volcanic landscapes, dramatic black sand beaches, and dramatic coastal views on this scenic route.
- **Caminho Real da Calheta (Royal Calheta Trail):** (Moderate difficulty) This historical trail along the south coast offers

stunning ocean views, a glimpse into Madeira's rich heritage, and charming traditional villages. Hike past old mills
and wineries, and soak up the island's cultural charm on
this moderately difficult route.

Remember, this is just a selection of some of Madeira's many
incredible hiking trails. With a little research, you can find the
perfect hike to match your interests, fitness level, and desired
level of challenge.

By using the provided information and maps as a starting
point, you can embark on an unforgettable hiking adventure in
Madeira, exploring the island's diverse landscapes, immersing
yourself in its natural beauty, and becoming a responsible
steward of this remarkable destination.

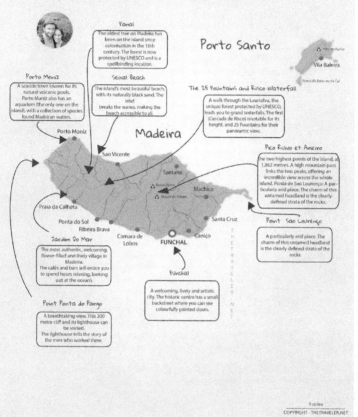

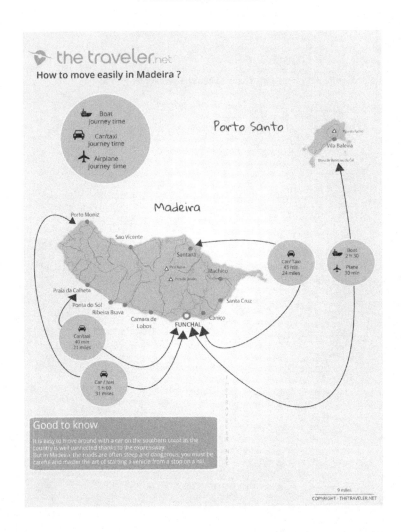

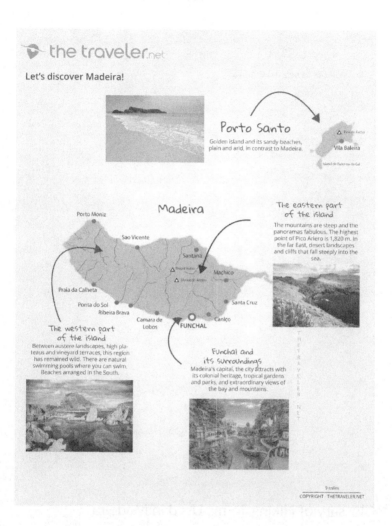

the traveler.net

Let's discover Madeira!

Porto Santo

Golden island and its sandy beaches, plain and arid, in contrast to Madeira.

Δ Pico do Facho
Vila Baleira

Island de Baixo ou de Cal

Madeira

Porto Moniz

Sao Vicente

Santana

Δ Pico do Areeiro

Δ Pico de Arieiro

Machico

Praia da Calheta

Ponta do Sol
Ribeira Brava
Camara de Lobos

Santa Cruz

Caniço

FUNCHAL

The eastern part of the island

The mountains are steep and the panoramas fabulous. The highest point of Pico Ariero is 1,820 m. In the far East, desert landscapes and cliffs that fall steeply into the sea.

The western part of the island

Between austere landscapes, high plateaus and vineyard terraces, this region has remained wild. There are natural swimming pools where you can swim. Beaches arranged in the South.

Funchal and its surroundings

Madeira's capital, the city attracts with its colonial heritage, tropical gardens and parks, and extraordinary views of the bay and mountains.

THE TRAVELER NET

9 miles
COPYRIGHT · THETRAVELER.NET

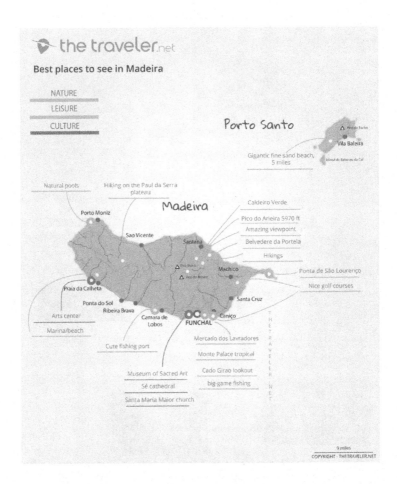

Glossary of Hiking Terms Used in Madeira

As you explore Madeira's diverse hiking trails, you might encounter some unfamiliar terms. Here's a handy glossary to help you navigate the island's hiking scene with confidence:

- **Levada (Levadas):** These are man-made irrigation channels that wind their way through the island's mountains and valleys. Levada walks are some of Madeira's most popular hikes, offering scenic walks alongside these historic water-courses.
- **Vereda (Veredas):** These are traditional hiking trails that traverse Madeira's mountains, forests, and coastlines. Veredas can range in difficulty from easy strolls to challenging ascents.
- **Miradouro (Miradouros):** These are viewpoints offering breathtaking panoramic vistas of the island's landscapes. Many levada walks and veredas incorporate miradouros along the route, providing opportunities to admire the scenery.
- **Laurissilva Forest:** This is a UNESCO World Heritage Site covering large parts of Madeira. It's a relic of ancient laurel forests and boasts a unique ecosystem with endemic flora found nowhere else on Earth.
- **Masīr (Path):** This is the Arabic word for "path" and is commonly used to refer to hiking trails in Madeira.
- **Fajã (Fajãs):** These are flat, fertile areas of land formed by lava flows reaching the sea. Some fajãs are accessible by hike and offer unique coastal landscapes.
- **Barranco (Barrancos):** These are deep ravines or gorges carved by erosion. Hiking trails sometimes lead through dramatic barrancos, offering a glimpse of Madeira's rugged terrain.
- **Pico (Pico):** This is the Portuguese word for "peak." Many of Madeira's mountains are referred to as "picos," including Pico Ruivo, the island's highest point.
- **Calhau (Calhaus):** These are pebble beaches, often made

up of smooth, black volcanic stones. Madeira's coastline boasts numerous calhaus, offering a unique alternative to sandy beaches.

· **Paul (Paul):** This refers to a plateau or high, flat area within the mountains. Some levada walks traverse these pauls, offering scenic vistas and a different perspective of the island's topography.

By understanding these terms, you'll be well-equipped to navigate Madeira's hiking trails, appreciate the island's unique landscapes, and have a more enriching hiking experience. So lace up your boots, grab your map, and get ready to explore!

Useful Websites and Resources for Madeira Hikers.

Planning a hiking adventure in Madeira requires a bit of research to ensure you choose the right trails, understand difficulty levels, and stay informed about safety precautions. Here are some valuable online resources to bookmark before you embark on your Madeiran exploration:

Official Websites:

· **Madeira Regional Tourism Authority:** https://visitmad eira.com/en/ - This official website provides a wealth of information on Madeira, including dedicated sections on hiking trails, levada walks, and downloadable maps.
· **Instituto das Florestas e da Conservação da Natureza (Forestry and Nature Conservation Institute):** https://if cn.madeira.gov.pt/ - This website, managed by the govern-ment agency responsible for nature conservation in Madeira, provides information on protected areas, hiking permits

(required for some trails), and trail conditions.

Hiking Apps and Maps:

- **Wikiloc:** https://www.wikiloc.com/ - This popular app offers a vast library of user-generated hiking trails worldwide, including Madeira. Download offline maps, access trail descriptions, and read reviews from other hikers.
- **ViewRanger:** https://my.viewranger.com/ - Another excellent app featuring downloadable maps, GPS navigation, and user-generated trail information for Madeira.
- **Maps.me:** https://maps.me/ - This free app allows you to download detailed offline maps of Madeira, including many hiking trails.

Hiking Blogs and Websites:

- **Walks in Madeira:** https://visitmadeira.com/en/what-to-do/nature-seekers/activities/hiking/ - This website offers detailed descriptions of various hiking trails in Madeira, with difficulty ratings, GPS tracks, and stunning photos to help you choose the perfect hike.
- **Island Life Madeira:** https://www.madeiraislandlife.com/ - This blog by a local resident provides insightful articles and recommendations on hiking in Madeira, including tips on gear, transportation, and hidden gems.
- **Madeira Hikers:** https://www.facebook.com/groups/madeira.walking/ - Join this active Facebook group to connect with fellow Madeira hikers, ask questions, and share experiences.

Weather Resources:

- **Instituto Português do Mar e da Atmosfera (Portuguese Institute for Sea and Atmosphere):** https://www.ipma.pt/pt/ - This website provides the latest weather forecasts for Madeira, essential for planning your hikes and ensuring you're prepared for changing conditions.
- **Windguru:** https://www.windguru.cz/ - This website offers detailed wind forecasts, valuable information for planning coastal hikes or hikes at higher elevations.

Additional Resources:

- **Lonely Planet Madeira:** https://www.lonelyplanet.com/portugal/madeira - This popular travel guidebook features a comprehensive section on hiking in Madeira, with detailed trail descriptions, maps, and additional travel tips.
- **Madeira Hiking Holidays:** https://madeirawalkingholidays.com/ - This tour operator specializes in guided hiking tours in Madeira. Their website offers valuable information on various trails and hiking experiences.

By utilizing these online resources, you can plan your Madeira hiking adventure with confidence. Researching trails, understanding difficulty levels, and staying informed about weather conditions will ensure you have a safe, enjoyable, and unforgettable experience exploring the island's breathtaking landscapes.

Made in United States
Orlando, FL
30 May 2024